2.25

UNDERSTANDING LITERATURE

UNDERSTANDING LITERATURE

BY

ROBIN MAYHEAD

Senior Lecturer in English, University of Lagos

CAMBRIDGE

AT THE UNIVERSITY PRESS

1965

PUBLISHED BY
THE SYNDICS OF THE CAMBRIDGE UNIVERSITY PRESS
Bentley House, 200 Euston Road, London, N.W. 1
American Branch: 32 East 57th Street, New York, N.Y. 10022
West African Office: P.O. Box 33, Ibadan, Nigeria

©

CAMBRIDGE UNIVERSITY PRESS
1965

Printed in Great Britain at the University Printing House, Cambridge
(Brooke Crutchley, University Printer)

CONTENTS

PART I

1. WHY STUDY LITERATURE?

This is a book about understanding literature. It would therefore be a good idea for us to begin by facing the question why literature should be considered worth understanding at all. English literature, with which we shall be mainly concerned in this book, is, as we all know, a 'Subject'. That is to say, it is taught in schools and universities and prescribed for examinations. There is little doubt that for a depressingly large number of students and former students this is a sufficient answer to our question. Literature, for them, is approached or remembered purely as a means to an end—the passing of examinations and the benefits thereof.

Now we cannot escape the fact that there are such things as examinations; nor can we, within the scope of this book, consider whether literature is or is not a proper 'Subject' for them. What we should do, however, is remind ourselves that no great writer ever designed his work to be potential matter for the examiners of posterity. Imagine Shakespeare writing *Hamlet* or Dickens *Great Expectations* with public examinations in mind! Still, as literature does indeed figure in examinations, and since it is presumably desirable to pass them, we might do well to explore an approach to literature that could combine enhanced possibilities of examination success with something far more profoundly and permanently valuable.

We may at this point ask ourselves why literature, in any case, should be regarded as important by examining bodies and educational institutions. The answer is simply that literature has been found over the centuries to have certain important kinds of value for human beings. One of these kinds of value has to do with the medium which literature employs: the medium of language.

All literature uses language, but by no means everything that is

1-2

written can be called literature. If that seems a fatuously obvious remark, it is none the less meant to carry a point. The world of today is flooded with writing of one kind or another. Every literate person is daily exposed to the onslaught of the printed word in various forms—newspapers, police notices, advertisements, forms to be filled in, magazines in doctors' waiting-rooms or left behind in trains, and so on. A great deal of this mass of print has an important or sometimes essential function. One example of an important function is the part played in the world by good journalism. Consider the following passage, which concerns itself with the successful setting-up of a direct line of communication between Russia and America, giving clear and concise information about a fact of the utmost potential significance:

THE HOT LINE linking the Kremlin with the White House went into service yesterday morning, one day ahead of schedule.

The American Embassy in Moscow said the Russians had set today as the opening date but tests had gone faster than expected.

The line will enable American and Soviet leaders to communicate quickly in a crisis, thus reducing the risk of war by accident. Teleprinter messages will be run regularly both on the teleprinter line and on a reserve radio circuit.

So far no one could have any reasonable objections to this piece of straightforward and informative journalistic writing. But what follows in the very next paragraph of the passage is much less encouraging:

In London the Foreign Office said Britain had welcomed the line as something with which Britain might in due course wish to be associated.

Gone are the clarity and point of the preceding sentences. In their place is a lamentable and vague verboseness. Whether this is the fault of the journalist or the Foreign Office spokesman we cannot be completely sure, though there is a distinct suggestion of a slightly embarrassed official not wishing to commit himself too far. Whatever the case may be, the sentence is deplorable. Why the clumsy and infelicitous repetition of 'Britain', for one thing? Why not 'Britain had welcomed the line as something with which *she* might in due course wish to be associated'? Yet that alteration does not go to the root of the trouble. Our real quarrel is with the words 'might in due course wish to be associated'. What exactly is this supposed to mean? We can accept the indeterminate 'might' as expressing a legitimate reluctance to make hasty decisions, but what of the other words? How long a time is meant to be conveyed by the phrase 'in due course'? What are we to suppose may happen to make the 'course' become '*due*'? And exactly what degree of co-operation is indicated by the words 'wish to be associated'? There is no answer to any of these questions, the truth being that the sentence is a tissue of clichés, stock official phrases designed to cover the absence of anything significant to say.

It may be argued that such a way of using language has its recognized place in what is called international diplomacy. Perhaps it has, though there is something laughable in its application to a scheme meant to promote *clarity* of international understanding! (Will the teleprinter messages sent on the line be equally vague and 'diplomatic'?) Whatever allowances we may or may not be disposed to make, however, such a mode of writing is very different from the way in which language is used in literature.

Equally remote from the literary use of language is the following specimen, this time from an advertisement for what claims to be a rather special kind of chewing gum. Under a drawing which depicts indubitably upper-class men and women with indubitably upper-class faces and clothes, at a fashionable race meeting, come the words 'CERTAINLY NOT', and then this:

Clearly, no one in his senses would use chewing gum at a time and place such as this.

However there are times and places where the use of chewing gum can be most beneficial; in fact its discreet use is a mark of tact and consideration for others as it is a definite aid to oral hygiene.

xxxxxx chewing gum is especially made for such people. Its ingredients are carefully selected throughout. . . .

5

The rest of the advertisement does not concern us. What does concern us is the quality of the writing. Possibly some readers may be a little surprised at my questioning it. 'The passage may not be *literature*,' they will perhaps say, 'but at any rate it is quite respectable English.' It does have the appearance of being 'good' English, the English of the educated person; in fact the English of the kind of person depicted in the drawing. This is because of the audience to which the advertisement is addressed. The advertiser wishes to sell his product both to people of the class depicted in the drawing and to people who aspire to belong to that class. In order to impress this audience, and thus promote the sale of the product, the advertiser makes a show of appealing to eminently rational and civilized standards of conduct—the standards of the educated person. Yet few genuinely educated people can have read that advertisement more than once without feeling that there is something wrong.

To what can this be traced? Is it simply that the advertisement in question employs what we call 'snob appeal', making the reader feel that if he uses xxxxxx chewing gum he will be thoroughly fashionable and upper-class? This will probably account for some of the discomfort; but an advertisement is after all designed to play upon the reader's susceptibilities, and although we may often laugh at the ways in which this is done, they do not seem quite enough to account for our present uneasy feeling.

No, the root of the trouble is in the seemingly impeccable language itself. There is nothing much wrong with the first sentence or two. We recognize the advertiser's technique in his assumption of sharing rational and civilized standards with the educated reader ('Clearly, no one in his senses...', 'its discreet use is a mark of tact and consideration for others...'), but we need not feel that there is anything seriously amiss with the language. It is when we come to the third paragraph that we put our fingers on the real weakness. 'xxxxxx chewing gum is especially made *for such people*.' To whom do the words 'such people' refer? They cannot refer to 'no one in his senses', since they are plural. Nor can they refer back to 'others', as the meaning makes this impossible. There is in fact no explanation to justify this piece of sloppy writing. Throwing syntax overboard is the only way to give 'such people' any meaning. By these words the writer of the advertisement presumably meant 'people who subscribe to the rational and civilized standards shared by the advertiser and the educated reader'. Alternatively (or, more probably, in addition) he meant 'people like those depicted in the drawing'. Whichever construction of his meaning we choose, we are abandoning the attempt to refer back the words 'such people' to anything that could justify them. 'Such people' can only mean 'people such as these' or 'people such as those'; and there is nothing earlier in the passage to answer the questions 'Such as *whom*?' or 'Such as *which*?'

It is possible to exaggerate the importance of tricks played upon one by advertisements. They have come to stay, whether we like their tactics or not, as part of the modern world's economy. Yet it is precisely in this that a danger lies. When one is being continually exposed to the kind of thing represented by the specimen we have been examining, there is a risk that one's whole idea of what language can do may be debased. The same thing goes for our example of Foreign Office jargon, whether or not a spokesman of that institution was actually guilty of it. Our great objection to such pieces of writing is that, in them, language is being used *without precision*. The language of any country is a precious possession, and, like all precious possessions, needs to be cared for. If we think of language in this way, we may feel that the perpetrators of the offences we have been scrutinizing are guilty men—guilty of an offence against part of their heritage.

A number of readers of this book may complain that English is not, in any real sense, their mother tongue, and thus cannot convincingly be referred to as part of their heritage. Yet is not this in itself a challenge? Is not a nation which has adopted English, either in whole or in part, for the conduct of its affairs, aware of special responsibilities towards the tool it has chosen? Does such a nation

7

not wish English to be a precision instrument rather than a collection of vague gestures?

We are now able to pinpoint one of the important kinds of value possessed by literature: it helps to preserve the precision and therefore the vitality of language. Notice that I say 'language', rather than 'the language it uses'. When a man is bilingual, sloppy habits acquired in the use of one of the languages he speaks will probably lead to similar offences in his handling of the other. For a nation which has adopted English for public and official matters, proper care for English should also mean proper care for its indigenous tongue or tongues. The greater part of this book will be concerned to show how literature uses language, and why it is possible to apply the words 'precision' and 'vitality' to the effect it has upon its medium.

This, however, is only one of the kinds of value literature has for human beings. Equally important is the fact that literature is meant to be enjoyed. The word 'enjoyment' is commonly misused; or perhaps not so much misused as employed in an unduly limited sense. Many readers may think of 'enjoyment' in terms of its more obvious forms: sport, dancing, the cinema. They will argue that such kinds of enjoyment are desirable because they make for relaxation, distracting one from the monotony or strain of day-to-day concerns. Now, there is nothing to be said against this view, provided that its supporters are willing to admit the possibility of other and additional kinds of enjoyment. To enjoy oneself means to have a sense of the joy of living; and this does not necessarily involve shutting down or restricting the activity of the mind. Indeed, that sense of the fullness and abundance of living that constitutes the most intense kind of enjoyment cannot be attained unless the mind is as much exercised as the other faculties.

That statement, like earlier ones in the chapter, may seem a pious platitude. It is none the less deliberate. In newly independent countries still undergoing change from a post-colonial phase to true autonomy, there is always the danger that exercise of the mind may tend to be popularly associated mainly with the educational routine followed in pursuit of a 'European post', and that it will not be thought of as having anything even remotely to do with 'enjoying oneself' once the educational goal and its consequent monetary benefits have been reached. It is partly to combat this tendency that the governments of many such countries have established arts councils, academies, and similar bodies to promote the knowledge of artistic and intellectual matters of both local and international importance. No praise can be too high for these ventures; but they will be disastrously handicapped if most people who have been to secondary school and university think of the enjoyment of leisure as something in which the mind plays little or no part.

Literature *is* to be enjoyed. It *does* make for relaxation; it *does* bring distraction from the monotony or strain of day-to-day concerns. But it does these things in ways from which mental laziness is quite remote. It relaxes by exercising, bringing into play faculties of the mind that would otherwise lie dormant. It distracts, not by offering a cowardly escape from the business of living, but by making living fuller and more meaningful. Literature can take us out of the track of weary routine, by leading us to understand something of that whole vast body of human living in which our day-to-day concerns have their place.

In countries which have gregarious societies, societies that think of leisure-time activity as something pursued in a group rather than in private, there is often to be found a certain contempt for the man who would rather sit at home and read than join, when summoned for a 'drive around' or some such diversion, in the merrymaking of his fellows. It is not uncommon in West Africa to hear a preference for solitary activity described as 'selfishness'. Now, a gregarious society is not necessarily anti-literary. Indeed, it tends to favour the development of a particular literary form—the drama. There is no doubt, however, that in such a society the idea of sustained reading for any purpose other than the passing of examinations still needs defence.

9

It cannot be too emphatically stated that reading is only in a most limited and unimportant sense a 'private' activity. A man reading silently is, in one way, 'alone', even though the room may be full of people, since he is doing something in which other persons present are taking no part. But it would be absurd to maintain that for this reason his activity must be despised as a sign of his wishing to shut himself away from the 'real world', or as a waste of the time he ought to be spending talking and laughing with his fellows. On the contrary, the reading of good literature can bring a man more closely into contact with the 'real world' than he could ever have been brought without a degree of personal experience for which the span of most lives is insufficient. And because of this, literature, far from making a man anti-social, can equip him to lead his life among his fellows with an adequacy, satisfaction, and understanding he would not otherwise have known.

At this point the sceptical person may ask 'What do you mean by talking about "the real world", and what, for that matter, do you mean by the word "literature"?' Let us start with the second question. Strictly speaking, 'literature' means anything written. In this sense, a physics text-book can be called 'literature'. We shall be concerned in the present book, however, with what is known as '*imaginative literature*'. A simple definition of imaginative literature could be that it is made up of poems, plays, short stories, and novels. Biographies and autobiographies, works of history, travel, and adventure, philosophical treatises, essays on social, religious, political, or even literary topics, many books by famous scientists— these can and often do deserve to be called literature by reason of a certain status and permanence given to them usually by a combination of the intrinsic importance or interest of their subject-matter and the mastery with which it is handled by the author. But, whatever the powers of imagination incidentally revealed in them, they are not what we mean by imaginative literature.

Trying to say what we do mean by imaginative literature takes us back to the first of our two questions: 'What do you think you mean by talking about "the real world"?' Let us consider the contrast between fact and fiction—between a work of biography and a novel, for example. It is obvious that the biography concerns the 'real world' in a very ordinary sense. It is about a person who really lived, about things he or she actually did or said, about the whole period and society in which the person moved—all this built up with as strict a regard for historical fact as the conscientious biographer can muster. A novel, on the other hand, concerns *invented* characters, with *invented* sayings and doings. Thus a novel, again in a very ordinary sense, is *not* about the 'real world', and it is for this reason that one can still come across the person who condemns all novels as a waste of time.

So far our distinction between fact and fiction is a simple one; but complications arise when we begin to look more closely at both biography and fiction. Granted that a work of biography is about someone who actually lived, it is plain that there are bound to be places where the author's knowledge of 'what actually happened' will be incomplete, the extent of this incompleteness being often though not always connected with the stretch of years dividing the period in which the subject lived from the date at which the author is writing. Whatever its extent, such incompleteness must inevitably lead the biographer to speculation, hypothesis, making the most of the scanty material available—in a word, to *interpretation*.

Now take the case of the novelist. His invented characters move, speak, and think, in a world which often seems very real indeed. We can believe in the Casterbridge of Thomas Hardy and the London of Charles Dickens, even though they are remote from the period in which we live and may be exceedingly remote from our own experience as persons. Why then did Hardy not write a strictly historical account of some aspect of Casterbridge life? Why did Dickens not do the same for London, instead of filling his books with such a fantastic collection of fictitious characters? The answer is that both Hardy and Dickens had more to *say*, more to say *about life in general as they saw it*, than they could possibly have said had they restricted themselves to the painstaking documentation of fact. They are men who have looked long and hard at the life they knew; in consequence they have arrived at an *interpretation* of it. This interpretation is not a simple affair. It cannot be expressed in a sentence such as 'All human beings are governed by destiny', or 'I think that a lot of men thrive by sucking the life-blood out of other human beings'. Only through the unfolding of their stories, and the actions and interactions of their characters, can the interpretation be adequately conveyed. Invented stories and invented characters—because these inventions, products of the imaginations of Hardy and Dickens, body forth, in the richest and most delicate form they can find, what those writers have to say about life as they saw it.

The novelist, then, has seen something he believes to be true about human life, something he believes to be *real*. His imagination gets to work on the reality he has seen, and finally his sense of it issues in the form of a novel. Do we in some cases reject his interpretation, feeling that human life cannot be 'like that'? Perhaps we may; but only at our peril do we dismiss it as negligible. The world we live in is bewildering enough, in all conscience, yet we must remember that human life has never been a mainly easy, simple, and straightforward business. It has been the lot of the great imaginative writer, since what we know of the beginnings of literature, to see and face different aspects of this whole vast complexity we call human life, and to convey his interpretation of them as faithfully as possible to his audience. 'This', he tells us, 'is the reality I have seen.' And this is precisely why we declared, a few pages back, that the reading of good literature can bring a man more closely into contact with the 'real world' than he could ever have been brought without a degree of personal experience for which the span of most lives is insufficient. Whether a reader says 'I agree with this', or 'I feel that this writer is utterly mistaken in his view of human behaviour', the important thing is that his reading has made him aware of new ways of looking at life, whether he likes them or not. The book will have enlarged his experience, enlarged his sense of what life, for better or for worse, can be. The man who shuts the book at the last page will be a different man from the one who opened it, though he may be quite unconscious of the change.

When we say that the imaginative writer is concerned with human life, the reader will probably feel that this is altogether too frightening a proposition, too high-and-mighty a concern, for *him*. Perhaps it makes literature seem too sublime, too august, too cold and lofty. If so, a direct thrust at the reader is immediately called for. Literature is not about some abstract thing called 'life'. It is about *your* life.

This may at first strike the reader as absurd. What can *A Tale of Two Cities* tell us about the life of a schoolboy in Ceylon? What connection can be imagined to exist between Elizabeth Bennet and a Ghanaian schoolgirl? To a teacher who knows either Ceylon or Ghana at all well, those questions are not necessarily as stupid as they look. We do not propose, however, to attempt the interesting exercise of answering them, though some reflections in Chapters 2 and 5 may suggest ways and means. The important thing is not whether or not the reader can feel that the situation of a particular character in a novel or some striking reflection in a poem has a special significance for him because of some personal idiosyncrasy or circumstance, but whether or not he can feel that what he is reading has any significance for him as a human being *at all*. If he cannot feel this about any literature, if he really cannot think of it as anything other than a 'subject', utterly removed from his own personal experience of living in the world, he had better abandon its study as an entire waste of time.

It is here that the question of 'background' arises. As this will be dealt with in Chapter 2, only two observations need be made at this point: (*a*) undue stress on differences of background between, say, an African reader and a European lady-novelist, though doubtless well intentioned, can be exceedingly dangerous, as it often imposes unnecessary obstacles to understanding; (*b*) a person of

13

average intelligence and tolerable literacy, whatever his background, will generally be aware, however dimly, that human beings have a remarkable way of resembling one another, wherever they come from, and that what is thought or felt vividly by any individual, real or fictitious, is unlikely to be quite without relevance for him.

The imaginative writer, in one way or another, is interested in *people*, in their variety, in their speech and behaviour, in their thoughts, feelings, and sensations. This is true even if he is interested mainly in himself. For a lyric poet, preoccupied with an experience in which no person other than himself plays a part, is certainly preoccupied with a human being. We may often, in some of the very greatest poetry, be not much aware of this human element. Yet it is there all the same. It took a human being to think that the poem was worth writing at all; it is the utterance of a human being, meant to be read and understood by other human beings; and a poet or any other kind of writer who claims that because he talks about animals or machines or the countryside he is therefore not interested in human considerations is merely being hypocritical.

Because of this concern with the human, and because the languages humans use are inextricably bound up with the lives they lead, the imaginative writer has a greater than ordinary interest in the possibilities of language. We have already spoken of one of the kinds of value possessed by literature—that it helps to preserve the precision and therefore the vitality of language. Examples in later chapters will be chosen to illustrate just what those words 'precision' and 'vitality' can mean. But one topic had better be brought up now, so that it need not trouble us again—the subject of Style. The reason for starting that word with a capital letter will perhaps be apparent to the reader after a consideration of the following passage:

Cities given, the problem was to light them. How to conduct individual citizens about the burgess-warren, when once heaven had withdrawn its leading luminary? or—since we live in a scientific age—when once our spinning planet has turned its back upon the sun? The moon, from time to time, was doubtless very helpful; the stars had a cheery look among the chimney-pots; and a cresset here and there, on church and citadel, produced a fine pictorial effect, and, in places where the ground lay unevenly, held out the right hand of conduct to the benighted. But sun, moon, and stars abstracted or concealed, the night-faring inhabitant had to fall back—we speak on the authority of old prints—upon stable lanthorns two stories in height (ROBERT LOUIS STEVENSON, *Virginibus Puerisque*).

That piece of verbiage is concerned with the problem of street-lighting, though the reader whose encounters with English prose have not run to sharing in such gymnastics could be excused for not immediately realizing this. What sort of writing is this, in which we have 'when once heaven had withdrawn its leading luminary' instead of 'when the sun had set', and 'when once our spinning planet has turned its back upon the sun' rather than 'when night has fallen' or the even plainer 'when it is dark'? It cannot be too emphatically stated that a greater than ordinary interest in the possibilities of language does not mean *that* kind of thing. Such a way of playing about with words is mere bloated affectation, debilitating language rather than nourishing it. Twaddle of this sort is less likely to be admired and held up as a model of Style today than it was forty or even twenty years ago; but sinister echoes of the past can still be heard here and there, and the teacher who exhorts his pupils to write 'like that' has by no means entirely disappeared. One hopes that the selection committees dealing with books prescribed for public examinations will aid in his extinction by eliminating such things from their lists.

We have concluded that literature has, broadly speaking, three important kinds of value: it vitalizes language; it makes for enjoyment; it tells us things we would not otherwise have known about the humanity of which we form a part. We have also insisted that the reader must feel that what he is reading has something to do with *his* life. It is this last point that we shall discuss further in our next chapter.

2. LITERATURE AND PERSONAL EXPERIENCE

Literature, we have said, is not about some abstract thing called 'life'. It is about *your* life. In what ways can this be true?

We shall start our discussion with a very simple example. Here is a passage from the novel *Things Fall Apart* by the Nigerian author Chinua Achebe:

Some days later, when the land had been moistened by two or three heavy rains, Okonkwo and his family went to the farm with baskets of seed-yams, their hoes and matchets, and the planting began. They made single mounds of earth in straight lines all over the field and sowed the yams in them.

Yam, the king of crops, was a very exacting king. For three or four moons it demanded hard work and constant attention from cock-crow till the chickens went back to roost. The young tendrils were protected from earth-heat with rings of sisal leaves. As the rains became heavier the women planted maize, melons and beans between the yam mounds. The yams were then staked, first with little sticks and later with tall and big tree branches. The women weeded the farm three times at definite periods in the life of the yams, neither early nor late.

And now the rains had really come, so heavy and persistent that even the village rain-maker no longer claimed to be able to intervene. He could not stop the rain now, just as he would not attempt to start it in the heart of the dry season, without serious danger to his own health. The personal dynamism required to counter the forces of these extremes of weather would be far too great for the human frame.

And so nature was not interfered with in the middle of the rainy season. Sometimes it poured down in such thick sheets of water that earth and sky seemed merged in one grey wetness. It was then uncertain whether the low rumbling of Amadiora's thunder came from above or below. At such times, in each of the countless thatched huts of Umuofia, children sat round their mother's cooking fire telling stories, or with their father in his *obi* warming themselves from a log fire, roasting and eating maize. It was a brief resting period between the exacting and arduous planting season and the equally exacting but light-hearted month of harvests.

It is obvious that such a passage will have an immediate impact upon a large number of readers from West Africa, and also those from other parts of the continent. Those who have actually lived in rural areas will, in particular, experience 'the shock of recognition'— the sense of seeing vividly described something that belongs to their own lives, with a feeling of pleased surprise at realizing that the whole thing can be done as perfectly, as succinctly, as *that*. For such readers the immediate reaction will be 'Yes, this is something I know. It touches my life because I have seen it all myself'.

There is no doubt that a reader who can say this will be at a certain advantage over one who cannot. He will enjoy an intimacy of contact with the passage denied to those whose lives have not encompassed the sort of experience described. He will, in fact, experience the simplest kind of relation that can exist between literature and life.

We shall be returning to Achebe later in this chapter. Let us meanwhile imagine the same African reader's response to something a little different. This time the setting is the island of Ceylon, and the source is *The Village in the Jungle* by Leonard Woolf:

So she was left alone with Punchirala. He was an old man now, weak and diseased. After a while he became too feeble even to get enough food to keep himself alive. She took him into her hut. She had to find food now for him, as well as for herself, by searching the jungle for roots and fruit, and by sowing a few handfuls of grain at the time of the rains in the ground about the hut. He gave her no thanks; as his strength decayed, his malignancy and the bitterness of his tongue increased; but he did not live long after he came to her hut; hunger and age and parangi at last freed her from his sneers and his gibes.

The jungle surged over and blotted out the village up to the very walls of her hut. She no longer cleared the compound or mended the fence, the jungle closed over them as it had closed over the other huts and compounds, over the paths and tracks. Its breath was hot and heavy in the hut itself which it imprisoned in its wall, stretching away unbroken for miles. Everything except the little hut with its rotting walls and broken

17

tattered roof had gone down before it. It closed with its shrubs and bushes and trees, with the impenetrable disorder of its thorns and its creepers, over the rice-fields and the tanks. Only a little hollowing of the ground where the trees stood in water when rain fell, and a long little mound which the rains washed out and the elephants trampled down, marked the place where before had lain the tank and its land.

The village was forgotten, it disappeared into the jungle from which it had sprung, and with it she was cut off, forgotten. It was as if she was the last person left in the world, a world of unending trees above which the wind roared always and the sun blazed. She became one of the beasts of the jungle, struggling perpetually for life against hunger and thirst; the ruined hut, through which the sun beat and the rains washed, was only the lair to which she returned at night for shelter. Her memories of the evils which had happened to her, even of Babun and her life with him, became dim and faded. And as they faded, her childhood and Silindu and his tales returned to her. She had returned to the jungle; it had taken her back; she lived as he had done, understanding it, loving it, fearing it. As he had said, one has to live many years before one understands what the beasts say in the jungle. She understood them now, she was one of them. And they understood her, and were not afraid of her. They became accustomed to the little tattered hut, and to the woman who lived in it. The herd of wild pigs would go grunting and rooting up to the very door, and the old sows would look up unafraid and untroubled at the woman sitting within. Even the does became accustomed to her soft step as she came and went through the jungle, muttering greetings to them; they would look up for a moment, and their great eyes would follow her for a moment as she glided by, and then the heads would go down again to graze without alarm.

The African reader will hardly feel altogether at a loss when reading that passage. It is true that he will be accustomed to speaking of 'bush' rather than 'jungle'; true also that the words 'parangi' and 'tank' will puzzle him unless he sees them in the context of the whole novel. But he is, nevertheless, unlikely to feel that this 'world of unending trees above which the wind roared always and the sun blazed' is unimaginably remote from the world he knows himself.

A sense of congeniality based upon mere similarities of climate and vegetation, however, is in itself neither valuable nor very interesting. The reader who simply says to himself 'This jungle seems rather like the bush that I have seen' will not have gone far in the direction of full response to the passage. For the jungle itself, though of immense importance to the passage, accounts for only part of the total effect built up. The second paragraph, in which the onrush of what has often been called the 'jungle tide' is so tellingly described for us, only reveals its proper significance in the context of the two paragraphs which enclose it. In other words, the full import of the jungle for this passage cannot be grasped unless we link the onrush of vegetation and the obliteration of the village with the situation of the woman whose life becomes so intimately bound up with the whole process. Thus the jungle is important here only in so far as it is connected with a human experience.

What will our African reader make of this human experience? Will he say 'This is a lot of nonsense. I cannot imagine myself becoming a beast of the jungle like this woman. It has never happened to me. Nothing like it will ever happen to me. Therefore the whole thing is valueless'? Much of course depends upon differences between individual readers. Some are always more sceptical, less willing to be 'taken in', than others. It is probable, however, that the reader we have in mind will, in a manner of speaking, be 'taken in' by the passage. He may not believe that what has happened to the woman will ever happen to him; he will certainly hope that it never does. But because of a degree of familiarity in the setting, possibly also because of odds and ends of tales of the bush that may have come his way, he will be able temporarily to project himself into the woman's situation. He will without too much difficulty succeed in imagining *what it could be like* to have the kind of experience described.

It is clear that for such a reader the passage by Leonard Woolf must involve a more complex response than the one by Achebe. It will also be, for him, a more valuable kind of response, as it will have *enlarged* his experience. There is more to be said about all this. Before we can profitably say it, however, we must consider a few more examples. The next is a famous poem by William Wordsworth:

Behold her, single in the field,
Yon solitary Highland Lass!
Reaping and singing by herself;
Stop here, or gently pass!
Alone she cuts and binds the grain,
And sings a melancholy strain;
O listen! for the Vale profound
Is overflowing with the sound.

No Nightengale did ever chaunt
More welcome notes to weary bands
Of travellers in some shady haunt,
Among Arabian sands:
A voice so thrilling ne'er was heard
In spring-time from the Cuckoo-bird
Breaking the silence of the seas
Among the farthest Hebrides.

Will no one tell me what she sings?—
Perhaps the plaintive numbers flow
For old, unhappy, far-off things,
And battles long ago:
Or is it some more humble lay,
Familiar matter of today?
Some natural sorrow, loss, or pain,
That has been, and may be again?

What'er the theme, the Maiden sang
As if her song could have no ending;
I saw her singing at her work,
And o'er the sickle bending;—
I listened, motionless and still;
And, as I mounted up the hill,
The music in my heart I bore,
Long after it was heard no more.

Some aspects of our imaginary reader's response to this poem can be left until we come to discuss the question of 'background'. For the time being, let us examine the factors which make the poem, both for him and for almost any other kind of reader, less accessible than either of our prose passages. First of all comes a difficulty over the matter of *time*. The present tense used in the first and third stanzas seems to indicate that we should imagine ourselves, together with the poet, listening to the maiden's song *now*, *at this present time*. We seem intended to think of her actually singing as we read the poem. But the last stanza unexpectedly complicates things. Here is a switch to the past tense. It now appears that the poet has for some reason been cheating us. The whole experience of listening to the maiden's song now seems very obviously over and done with long before the writing of the poem, let alone our reading of it. What does the poet think he is doing?

The clue to the problem is contained in the last two lines:

> The music in my heart I bore,
> Long after it was heard no more.

The maiden's song has most certainly ceased actually to be heard by the time Wordsworth writes the poem; but it has made so deep an impression that it remains with him, it still seems *present* to him. This sense of carrying the music with him into the present, even though it is no longer physically audible, is what Wordsworth wishes us to share with him; and it is for this reason that he puts most of his poem in the present tense. And when, in the last stanza, the whole thing is suddenly revealed to us as having happened well away in the past, we are made to realize just how intense an experience it has been for him. If he can write about it like this, if he can arouse in us so vivid a sense that it is all actually going on, although it has in fact taken place a long time ago—then, we feel, he is really telling us the truth when he says:

> The music in my heart I bore,
> Long after it was heard no more.

We now have to confront a further difficulty. So far we have not mentioned the second stanza. Let us look at it now, and ask ourselves, once again, what the poet thinks he is doing:

21

No Nightengale did ever chaunt
More welcome notes to weary bands
Of travellers in some shady haunt,
Among Arabian sands:
A voice so thrilling ne'er was heard
In spring-time from the Cuckoo-bird
Breaking the silence of the seas
Among the farthest Hebrides.

Our first reaction may be that Wordsworth is merely using needlessly flowery language to tell us the simple fact that he was pleasantly struck by the girl's singing. We might even go on to accuse him of positive incompetence. If he really is concerned to make us see just how intense the experience has been for him, why should he distract our attention from the thing itself by bringing in thoughts of Arabia and the Hebrides? A geographically-minded reader might admit that mention of the Hebrides is not altogether irrelevant, since those islands, even the 'farthest' of them, are not so very distant from the Scottish Highlands. He might, on the other hand, still be at a loss to understand what the Arabian desert is doing in the poem.

One part of the answer is connected with the word 'solitary' in the first stanza. The 'solitary Highland Lass' is found 'single in the field', 'Reaping and singing by herself', cutting and binding the grain 'Alone'. We are further told that the field in which she is working is situated in a deep valley, a 'Vale profound', which is filled to overflowing with her song. There is evidently complete silence otherwise, for the reader who is imagined to be sharing the poet's experience is admonished to 'Stop here, or gently pass'. Whatever he does, he must not break the sense of enchantment born of the stillness of the valley and the girl's unawareness that anyone else is there. Solitude and a vast surrounding silence— these seem to be essential ingredients of the situation. We can now understand why 'the farthest Hebrides' have been brought in. This is not a question of geographical proximity. They are there in the poem because of their loneliness, and because of 'the silence of the seas' around them—a silence broken in spring-time by the voice of the cuckoo, just as the silence of 'the Vale profound' is broken only by the maiden's song. And from the solitude and silence of the sea to their equivalent on land, the solitude and silence of the desert, is not a difficult step for the mind to take. (The sea and the desert, indeed, seem curiously similar to one another, precisely because they are at opposite extremes.) In each case we have an impression of deep loneliness and silence, broken and relieved by a single 'thrilling' voice, be it that of a nightingale in some desert oasis, the cuckoo away in the Hebrides, or the girl reaping in the field. A chain of association, which starts with the words 'solitary' and 'single', holds all these things together.

I said that this would give us one part of the answer to the question of what Wordsworth is doing in the second stanza. To complete our investigation we must now look again at the third:

> Will no one tell me what she sings?—
> Perhaps the plaintive numbers flow
> For old, unhappy, far-off things,
> And battles long ago:
> Or is it some more humble lay,
> Familiar matter of today?
> Some natural sorrow, loss, or pain,
> That has been, and may be again?

That stanza is not in itself at all hard to grasp. Wordsworth does not know what the girl is singing about, and he speculates on the possible subject of her 'melancholy strain'. But there is something very interesting in the directions his speculation takes. You will observe that he considers two distinct sets of possibilities, with a third almost imperceptibly growing out of the second:

> (1) Perhaps the plaintive numbers flow
> For old, unhappy, far-off things,
> And battles long ago:

(i.e. perhaps her song concerns tragic historical events.)

> (2) Or is it some more humble lay,
> Familiar matter of today?

(i.e. perhaps her song has no such grand associations with the past, but concerns ordinary people and affairs of the present.)

> (3) Some natural sorrow, loss, or pain,
> That has been, and may be again?

The distinction between (1) and (2) is perfectly clear. It is the distinction between the past and the present. But (3) is not such a simple matter. It is of course quite easy to read it as though it were part and parcel of (2). If we do this, then we must take the 'natural sorrow, loss, or pain' to be the 'Familiar matter of today' about which the girl may or may not be singing. There is no harm in doing this, as it makes excellent sense; but one wonders why Wordsworth, if that was really his entire meaning, bothered to put a question mark after 'today' instead of a comma; so:

> Or is it some more humble lay,
> Familiar matter of today,
> Some natural sorrow, loss, or pain,
> That has been, and may be again?

He might even have used a semi-colon. As it stands, we cannot escape the odd feeling that Wordsworth is rather artfully opening up a third set of possibilities, which are certainly related to the 'Familiar matter of today', but which also take us a good deal further than the present as we usually think of it. Indeed, the last line of the stanza makes us think of the past and the possible future rather than 'today' in any ordinary sense:

> That *has been*, and *may be again*?

What comes out of all this? Surely it is the feeling that the usual simple distinctions between the past, the present, and the future, have been broken down. Wordsworth starts by thinking of the 'old, unhappy, far-off things' of the past. He moves from them to the 'Familiar matter of today'. But what he ends up with is what we may best call *the continuity of life itself*, a sense that what 'has been' and what 'may be again' are part of an eternally unfolding pattern which it is idle to attempt to divide up into past, present, and future.

24

Life, with its 'natural sorrow, loss, or pain', goes on, like the maiden's song, as if it 'could have no ending'; and, as Wordsworth listens to the singing, he seems to stand outside time altogether:

I listened, motionless and still;

And just as he stands outside the bounds of time, so he stands outside the bounds of space as well. His imagination is free to range from the field in the Scottish Highlands to the sands of Arabia, the desolate Hebrides, and back again. This sense of being, perhaps only briefly, beyond the confines of time and space, is the central experience recounted by the poem.

It will be seen that what we have carried out is a piece of fairly close analysis. Some readers may object that the analysis has been too *difficult*, that it has gone further in the direction of detail and subtlety than this particular stage of the book can warrant. Could it, however, have been very much more simple? The poem conveys, with point and precision, a subtle experience. No endeavour, therefore, to say what the poem is about, can help having its own difficulty and complexity.

What will the reader, from Africa or anywhere else, make of the subtle experience recounted by the poem? It is just possible that something not unlike it may have happened to him. More probably it will bring him something completely new, an experience he would not normally imagine himself having, but which may seem perfectly feasible after the reading. I say that it *may* seem perfectly feasible, as a lot depends upon the individual reader's willingness to accept the unfamiliar. Plainly, for our African reader alone, understanding the poem involves a great deal more than response to the extract from *The Village in the Jungle*. Placing oneself in the position of a woman reduced by circumstance to the level of a beast of the jungle may seem, on the face of things, quite as hard as imagining oneself standing outside the bounds of time and space. Yet, whatever the improbabilities in either case, the first of those two efforts of the imagination, for our African reader, will undoubtedly be the easier—partly because accidents of environment make the prose passage more immediately understandable to him; partly because, like any other reader, he will find the experience recounted in *The Solitary Reaper* far more complex.

To say that the experience recounted in the poem is complex, however, is not the same thing as saying that it is irrelevant to other people who are not poets. It is the intense experience of a human being, translated into language of point and precision. As such it has relevance for all human beings, whether they have themselves had anything like the experience or not. They will certainly have had the experience after reading the poem. And to those sceptics who may object that the business of sharing Wordsworth's experience is so much wasted effort, one can only assert, as weightily as one can, that the sense he evokes of standing outside the bounds of time and space is part of the business of being human; and that to reject it as valueless, whoever you are and whatever part of the world you come from, is to reject the possibility of enlarging your own experience of being human. Time and space are inextricably mixed up with our lives as humans. We tend to look upon both these things, especially time, in rather fixed and conventional ways. Wordsworth's poem gives us something new, vivid, and refreshing.

This discussion of *The Solitary Reaper* has been founded on the assumption that although few readers are likely to have had the same kind of experience as Wordsworth, the majority will not dismiss as inconceivable the possibility that something of the sort *might* happen to them. Our next example is of an entirely different order:

> CORDELIA. How does my royal lord? How fares your majesty?
> LEAR. You do me wrong to take me out o' the grave:
>   Thou art a soul in bliss; but I am bound
>   Upon a wheel of fire, that mine own tears
>   Do scald like molten lead.
> CORDELIA.   Sir, do you know me?
> LEAR. You are a spirit, I know: when did you die?
> CORDELIA. Still, still, far wide!

DOCTOR. He's scarce awake: let him alone awhile.
LEAR. Where have I been? Where am I? Fair daylight?
I am mightily abused. I should e'en die with pity,
To see another thus. I know not what to say.
I will not swear these are my hands: let's see;
I feel this pin prick. Would I were assured
Of my condition!
CORDELIA.   O, look upon me, sir.
And hold your hands in benediction o'er me.
No, sir, you must not kneel.
LEAR.   Pray, do not mock me:
I am a very foolish fond old man,
Fourscore and upward, not an hour more or less;
And, to deal plainly,
I fear I am not in my perfect mind.
Methinks I should know you and know this man;
Yet I am doubtful; for I am mainly ignorant
What place this is, and all the skill I have
Remembers not these garments, nor I know not
Where I did lodge last night. Do not laugh at me;
For, as I am a man, I think this lady
To be my child Cordelia.
CORDELIA.   And so I am, I am.
LEAR. Be your tears wet? yes, faith. I pray, weep not:
If you have poison for me, I will drink it.
I know you do not love me; for your sisters
Have, as I do remember, done me wrong:
You have some cause, they have not.
CORDELIA.   No cause, no cause.

We have now arrived at one of the greatest moments in the
whole of English literature—the moment in Act IV, Scene vii of
Shakespeare's *King Lear* when Cordelia speaks to her father for
the first time since their tragic separation in the first act. Cordelia
has been rejected for her honesty. Lear in turn has been rejected
by her falsely flattering, sugary-tongued sisters, Regan and Goneril.
Exposed to the terrors of darkness and tempest, he has known, for
the first time in his long life, what it is to suffer. He has felt at last
what the very poor feel; he has had an overwhelming vision of the

foulness and degradation to which humanity can descend. Finally he has known madness. Yet it is no ordinary madness. It is one of the many paradoxes of this great and terrifying but also consoling play that Lear loses his reason only in order to find it.

Here, in this scene, Lear lies asleep in the camp of the forces of the French king, Cordelia's husband. Before him stands the daughter so bitterly cast off, the daughter to whom he has once said:

> Better thou
> Hadst not been born than not to have pleased me better.

But this daughter harbours no rancour. Of her it is said, in Act IV, Scene iii, when the news has reached her of Lear's brutal treatment at the hands of her sisters:

> You have seen
> Sunshine and rain at once: her smiles and tears
> Were like, a better way: those happy smilets
> That play'd on her ripe lip seem'd not to know
> What guests were in her eyes; which parted thence
> As pearls from diamonds dropp'd. In brief,
> Sorrow would be a rarity most beloved,
> If all could so become it.

Sorrow and horror at what has befallen her father mingle with a radiant joy at the thought of being reunited with him. Now at last the moment has come. For a time Lear does not recognize her. Before he can know her, he must first know himself—know himself as he never did in the days of his headstrong, domineering, yet essentially childish pride:

> I am a very foolish fond old man,
> Fourscore and upward, not an hour more or less;
> And, to deal plainly,
> I fear I am not in my perfect mind.

Only now can the revelation come:

> Do not laugh at me;
> For, as I am a man, I think this lady
> To be my child Cordelia.

All that has happened before in the play lies behind this moment of truth. With these words the scales lift from the eyes of Lear; and to the anguish and darkness of madness and storm succeeds the scarcely believable dawn of reconciliation and forgiveness:

> I know you do not love me; for your sisters
> Have, as I do remember, done me wrong:
> You have some cause, they have not.
> CORDELIA.   No cause, no cause.

It is not likely that many people will have lived through any-thing at all closely resembling the experience of Lear or Cordelia, though life holds many surprises in the way of happiness and suffering. Most of us can say with Albany at the very end of the drama that we

> Shall never see so much, nor live so long.

But can we for that reason dismiss the experience which *King Lear* gives, as irrelevant to us, as having nothing to do with our lives? Of course not. This drama of wrong-headed obstinacy, suffering, bestiality, and redemption, has a meaning for us all. To deny its importance for oneself, merely because the accidents of one's personal life afford no parallels to the events of the drama, is to deny one's own humanity.

Maybe some readers will feel that it was unnecessary to insist on this. 'Shakespeare', they may say, 'is a Classic. We all know that his plays have a Universal Significance. Therefore all this talk about "One's own humanity" is superfluous.' It would indeed be comforting to think that it really *was* superfluous. There is plenty of reason to suppose, however, that Shakespeare's status as a Classic is far from being an advantage for him. Once you have said 'Classic' you are well on the way to saying 'Prescribed Author'; and once you have said 'Prescribed Author' you have invoked the bogey of examinations, Eng. Lit., and the cynicism and depression that all too often go with them. It is necessary to emphasize that no good will come of mouthing the words 'Universal Significance' unless

29

the student realizes that he belongs himself to the same universe in which Shakespeare's characters move; that the tale of Lear's suffering concentrates into dramatic form the suffering of humanity as a whole; and that to experience this drama is to learn more than one could ever have known otherwise about the humanity of which one is a tiny part.

The very greatest works of literature tend, like *King Lear*, to give one experiences that one would not think of oneself as conceivably undergoing in the course of actual life, but which yet have so profound an application to human life as a whole that they deeply affect one as an individual human creature. For our African reader, *King Lear* will in obvious ways be at the opposite extreme of familiarity from *Things Fall Apart*; but it will not for that reason have any less to say to him as a human being.

It is true, however, that the most familiar kind of relation between literature and personal experiences the reader may have had is a more general one. It involves neither extremely close approximation to actual personal experience, as in the case of the African reader of *Things Fall Apart*, nor extreme remoteness from actual personal experience, as would be the case with almost any reader of *King Lear*. For an illustration of this type of connection between our personal lives and the books we read, let us take a passage from the novel *Aaron's Rod*, by D. H. Lawrence:

'Oh!' exclaimed Millicent feverishly, instantly seized with desire for what she had not got, indifferent to what she had. Her eye ran quickly over the packages. She took one.

'Now!' she exclaimed loudly, to attract attention. 'Now! What's this?— What's this? What will this beauty be?'

With finicky fingers she removed the newspaper. Marjory watched her wide-eyed. Millicent was self-important.

'The blue ball!' she cried in a climax of rapture. 'I've got *the blue ball*.'

She held it gloating in the cup of her hands. It was a little globe of hardened glass, of a magnificent full dark blue colour. She rose and went to her father.

'It was *your* blue ball, wasn't it, father?'

'Yes.'

'And you had it when you were a little boy, and now I have it when I'm a little girl.'

'Ay,' he replied drily.

'And it's never been broken all those years.'

'No, not yet.'

'And perhaps it never will be broken?'

To this she received no answer.

'Won't it break?' she persisted. 'Can't you break it?'

'Yes, if you hit it with a hammer,' he said.

'Aw!' she cried. 'I don't mean that. I mean if you just drop it. It won't break if you drop it, will it?'

'I daresay it won't.'

'But *will* it?'

'I sh'd think not.'

'Should I try?'

She proceeded gingerly to let the blue ball drop. It bounced dully on the floor-covering.

'Oh-h-h!' she cried, catching it up. 'I love it.'

'Let *me* drop it,' cried Marjory, and there was a performance of admonition and demonstration from the elder sister.

But Millicent must go further. She became excited.

'It won't break,' she said, 'even if you toss it up in the air.'

She flung it up, it fell safely. But her father's brow knitted slightly. She tossed it wildly: it fell with a little splashing explosion: it had smashed. It had fallen on the sharp edge of the tiles that protruded under the fender.

'*Now* what have you done!' cried the mother.

The child stood with her lip between her teeth, a look, half of pure misery and dismay, half of satisfaction, on her pretty, sharp face.

'She wanted to break it,' said the father.

'No she didn't! What do you say that for!' said the mother. And Millicent burst into a flood of tears.

He rose to look at the fragments that lay splashed on the floor.

'You must mind the bits,' he said, 'and pick 'em all up.' He took one of the pieces to examine it. It was fine and thin and hard, lined with pure silver, brilliant. He looked at it closely. So—this was what it was. And this was the end of it. He felt the curious soft explosion of its breaking still in his ears. He threw his piece in the fire.

'Pick all the bits up,' he said. 'Give over! give over! Don't cry any more.'

For many English or American readers this passage will have a particularly authentic ring: Christmas Eve, the ornaments for decorating the Christmas tree, all the excitement of the Christmas season for childhood. Yet it would be too much to claim that the advantage they draw from personal associations (probably memories of their own childhood) is a very special or important one. The reader who has been brought up in a tropical climate, on the other hand, will not be accustomed to thinking of 'the sharp edge of the tiles that protruded under the fender', or anything like them, as part of the domestic scene he knows and remembers. He may or may not associate Christmas trees with his own experience of the season. But it would be absurd to declare that the absence of certain personal associations enjoyed by the English reader amounts to a serious disadvantage when it comes to understanding what the passage is really *about*. No intelligent reader is going to be alarmed because he has never seen a fender, or because there was never a Christmas tree in the house when he was young. Nor will an intelligent reader think that he is admitted to some very special understanding of the passage simply because he knows all about fenders and Christmas trees.

What is going on in the passage? As we shall see in Chapter 5, it is impossible to look for long at any passage in a good novel without reference to the whole. This passage from *Aaron's Rod* is no exception. It is not here our business to examine this novel. For our purposes it is enough to say that the episode described occurs in the first chapter, and that most of the action of the book takes place after the man, Aaron Sisson, has decided to go away and leave his family. This gives a clue to the meaning of the episode. It can be regarded simply as describing the behaviour of a wilful and impulsive little girl, over-excited as children can so often be on Christmas Eve. But there is more to it than that. The break between Aaron and his family is foreshadowed in this apparently slight domestic scene. The shattering of the blue ball points forward to the shattering of the family.

We can go further. If the family breaks up, it is because relations between its members are not what they should be. Tiny and perhaps apparently trivial things in the passage indicate the presence of tension:

'*Now* what have you done!' cried the mother.
The child stood with her lip between her teeth, a look, half of pure misery and dismay, half of satisfaction, on her pretty, sharp face.
'She wanted to break it,' said the father.
'No she didn't! What do you say that for!' said the mother. And Millicent burst into a flood of tears.

The tension does not come out only in the exchange between husband and wife. It is there also in the 'look, *half* of pure misery and dismay, *half* of satisfaction', on the child's face. Aaron is right. Millicent did want to break the blue ball, though she probably only half knew this. But however obscure her feelings may be to herself, she cannot help revealing a glint of satisfaction, as the ball lies shattered.

What is the reason for this satisfaction? It is because Millicent, in her childish way, feels a certain sense of triumph. She has somehow scored over her father; she has asserted herself against him, and won. Dimly, she has all the time known that this blue ball, though a mere ornament of no value in itself, has a significance for Aaron. It is a link with his youth, yet Millicent wants to possess it herself and then, possessing it completely, to destroy it. All the destructive power of *possessiveness* in personal relationships, even when exerted by a mere child, is implied in this simple piece of dialogue:

'It was *your* blue ball, wasn't it, father?'
'Yes.'
'And you had it when you were a little boy, and now I have it when I'm a little girl.'
'Ay,' he replied drily.
'And it's never been broken all those years.'
'No, not yet.'
'And perhaps it never will be broken?'
To this she received no answer.

And it is clear that the mother, despite her exclamation '*Now* what have you done!', is with her daughter and against her husband.

More could be said about this masterly piece of writing in the light of *Aaron's Rod* as a whole. For us, however, one central point is of great importance. It does not matter whether or not you can refer the episode and its setting back to things you have yourself actually seen or done. It also does not greatly matter whether or not there is something about the society in which you have grown up that makes it hard for you to imagine the incident occurring exactly as Lawrence has described it, even when due allowance has been made for small pieces of unfamiliarity in the setting. What does matter is the fact that everybody, at some time or other, and very often in childhood, knows what family tensions are like. This is the universal significance of the passage. You may come from the happiest and most harmonious home, but it is practically inconceivable that you will have grown up without seeing, if only in some other family, something that in a general way is *like* the episode from *Aaron's Rod*. The probability that it had no connection with decorations for a Christmas tree is beside the point. It only matters that you should be aware of the episode, not merely as 'an incident in a book', but as something typical of life itself, wherever it is lived.

I have said that this passage illustrates the most usual kind of relation between literature and life. It involves neither extreme closeness to personal experience (though it is always possible that for some readers the approximation to what they have actually lived through may be a very near one), nor unimaginable remoteness. We have looked at examples of both closeness and remoteness, together with pieces of writing that show us intermediate stages. Despite the differences between them, there is one thing which can be said about all five, and it can also be said about literature as a whole: an art which concerns itself with people, as literature does, *must, in one way or another, have a bearing upon the business of living one's own life.*

We now have to confront the spectre of 'background', already briefly conjured up in Chapter 1. I call it a spectre because it is usually sinister, often a nuisance, and because there is something insubstantial about it. For the time being, however, we must assume that it has flesh and blood, and look it boldly in the face.

What, to begin with, do we mean by the question of 'background'? Perhaps it may best be formulated like this: every reader has grown up in a certain environment. This means that he will have acquired certain ways of looking at life which are typical of that environment. These will be connected with customs, social and religious codes and conventions, and also the ordinary necessities of living. When he comes into contact with a literature that has sprung from a different environment, particularly when it belongs to a different continent, he is baffled and bewildered, because the literature assumes ways of looking at life which are quite different from those he has acquired. It is 'foreign' to him.

Now, it would be idle to pretend that there is no truth in any of this. Problems undoubtedly do exist, but the important thing is to decide what they really are. One kind of supposed 'problem' must be dismissed right away, and in this connection it will be useful to return to Wordsworth's *The Solitary Reaper*. The song which so captivates the poet is sung by a 'Highland Lass'. He thinks, in the second stanza, of 'Arabian sands', and

> the Cuckoo-bird
> Breaking the silence of the seas
> Among the farthest Hebrides.

And, we might add, he also mentions 'spring-time'. Will a student in, say, Ghana or Ceylon or Malaya, know why the maiden is called a 'Highland Lass'? If his geography lessons have made 'Arabian sands' comprehensible to him, will he know just where the Hebrides are? Will he know what a cuckoo sounds like? And what will 'spring-time' mean to someone from a tropical climate?

There are two ways of answering the worried reader or teacher who feels that his own or his students' possible ignorance of these things is a frightful obstacle to understanding the poem. The first

2-2

thing to say is simply that if the student is genuinely put out, then a very few minutes of explanation will clear things up for him. By all means let information be given. There is always a place for this, though the kind of value it has must not be exaggerated. For the second thing to say is that the student must on no account be led to attach too much importance to the information he has received about the Scottish Highlands, the Hebrides, and the cuckoo-bird. It is just possible (though I have my doubts) that locating the Scottish Highlands and the Hebrides on a map of the British Isles *might* conceivably be of some kind of use. There is no doubt, however, that an account of the habits and nesting characteristics of the cuckoo would be ridiculously out of place. And yet there are zealous teachers who, incredible though it may seem, think it necessary to go into that kind of thing. The only thing that matters about the cuckoo, as far as this poem is concerned, is that it has a distinctive call, and that it is heard in the season called spring, which heralds a change from the cold season called winter. The Scottish Highlands are significant only in so far as they provide the immediate setting for the poem; and as for the 'Arabian sands' and 'the farthest Hebrides', the only thing worth pointing out about them is that they are very distant and different from one another, the important qualification of this being that *they share associations of solitude*. In other words, one must occupy oneself with what really matters in a poem, not with what is incidental. In case this sort of insistence seems unnecessary, might I be allowed to recall the familiar kind of teacher who really appears to suppose that something is gained by the student of Wordsworth's poetry from his having coloured photographs of those eternal daffodils or lantern slides of the Lake District displayed before him? The fact that the student has never seen or may never be likely to see a daffodil is of limited significance. What he does need to be told before he reads the poem is that the daffodil *is a flower*. The teacher might go on to say that it is a bright yellow flower with a head that nods in the breeze, and that it grows in great groups; but these facts can and should be deduced from the poem itself. Information of this kind, if given in excess, may run the risk of being taken as a substitute for first-hand response to the poem.

It must be emphasized that literature has the power to generate its own understanding. In a complex structure, like *The Solitary Reaper*, the parts are inter-determining. That is to say, one element in the poem will be determined by and will itself determine every other element, so that an attentive reader will catch the right effect from the context. Thus the important point that 'Arabian sands' and 'the farthest Hebrides' share associations of solitude can be elicited from their place in the context of the whole poem. It has, nevertheless, to be admitted that certain words, like 'Arabian' and 'daffodils', conjure up particular associations which are likely to be more immediately accessible to an English reader than to our hypothetical reader from West Africa—associations which to the latter can only be made real by a wider and richer acquaintance *with imaginative literature in general*. The reader who knows his Shakespeare, and into whose sensibility certain Shakespearian passages have been more or less unconsciously received, will hardly be able to help recalling 'All the perfumes of Arabia', and 'daffodils that come before the swallow dares'. The reader of Wordsworth who is unfamiliar with *Macbeth* and *The Winter's Tale*, or who may have read those plays without the words in question having passed into his stock of associations, will inevitably respond to the poems in a more limited way. There is little that the teacher can do about this, beyond suggesting a few of the likely associations in works accessible to the student, and, what is far more important, encouraging him to read as widely as possible, and to regard literature, not as being made up of unrelated units, but as a whole, in which individual works and individual authors may be mutually illuminating, even though often historically remote from one another.

It is presumably not suggested that a European reader of Achebe's *Things Fall Apart* is debarred from an understanding of that novel by reason of his never having seen a yam. Yet things as silly as that are constantly being said about the non-European student of English literature, and are earnestly debated in common rooms and at meetings of English teachers' associations into the bargain. To the student who suffers from such half-baked nonsense, one can only say 'Be on your guard against the teacher who tells you that you cannot understand *I Wandered Lonely as a Cloud* or anything else in English literature without a whole assortment of aids that have nothing to do with literature at all. The chances are that he doesn't really understand the poem himself.' To the teacher one must say, in an imploring tone, 'Give only such explanatory information as is *absolutely necessary*. Make sure that you know what the work of literature in question is really about before you start discussing it, and *never* treat it in such a way as to make the student feel that it is distant from the world he knows.'

What may be called the 'basic information aspect' of this background question, then, can be written off as barely amounting to a genuine problem. We have, however, agreed that problems do exist, and that differences in environment between the reader and the work of literature may give rise to certain difficulties. The biggest of these difficulties, so big that all others are of small importance beside it, has already been considered in Chapter 1. In fact the whole of the first chapter has been devoted to an attempt to deal with it. It is the difficulty of making people believe that good literature is worth reading at all. Basically, this is not a question involving any distinctive difference between non-European and European. Exposed to the clamour of the cheaper forms of commercial entertainment, the European or American is in some respects less likely than his Asian or African counterpart to think literature worthy of his attention. Nevertheless, quite apart from the fact that non-European countries are by no means insulated from the racket of 'pop' values, it is certainly true that in some of them, especially those which have not already a strong literary tradition of their own, a case for literature has to be made. To say that in such countries literature has not been part of the life of even the educated to any great extent is to say nothing against those countries—though it may well be saying something against the former expatriate rulers of some of them. But, as we have observed, governments have taken the lead in recognizing the importance of literary and artistic values in general. It is the duty of those who teach in their countries to support them.

This very fundamental problem, strangely enough, is not one of those habitually thought of by people who debate the topic of 'background'. It cannot, accordingly, be properly counted as one of the manifestations of our 'spectre'. One of those manifestations, the 'basic information' aspect, has already been disposed of. What therefore remains?

There remains what we said in our attempted formulation of the 'background' question: that a reader, when he comes into contact with the literature of an environment different from his own, will be baffled and bewildered, because the literature assumes ways of looking at life which are quite different from those he has acquired. How much real truth is there in this? There is a limited truth in it; but, as in the case of 'basic information', it must not be exaggerated. Both students and teachers should remember that a great deal of English literature needs no less explanation to the Englishman than it does to the Canadian or Nigerian. For most English readers the Highlands and the Hebrides are as much a mere geographical expression as 'the Arabian sands'. Elizabethan ideas regarding Kingship and the Natural Order are as foreign to the Englishman as to the African—perhaps more foreign—and knowledge of them is essential to a proper understanding of *King Lear* or *Macbeth*. Yet, as every sensitive modern Shakespearian critic has been at pains to insist, knowledge of those ideas cannot be looked at as being more than an aid towards understanding. It must never be taken as a substitute for the plays themselves. The same may be said of the odds and ends of knowledge relating to social customs, forms, conventions, and so on, which the teacher may feel are really essential for our African reader of English literature.

There is a close parallel for the reader whose native tongue is not

39

English between the question of 'background' knowledge and that of reading-speed. Granted that the non-native speaker of English does, at any rate for a considerable time, tend to read more slowly than an Englishman or an American, one must nevertheless deplore excessive and *unwarranted* slowness. By this I mean the self-imposed slowness resulting from the reader's conviction that, because English is not his native language, he cannot conceivably see in a page of English writing the meaning that an Englishman will see in it, unless he brings to his reading the most intense and laborious effort. Reading-speed does of course vary from one person to another, but in most students at universities and in the higher forms of secondary schools overseas it is far closer to that of a native speaker of English than they are often led to believe—or rather, it would be, if only they could be prevented from acquiring an inferiority complex about the language. Naturally, carelessness in reading is not to be encouraged. A proper balance has to be established, the reader accepting the fact that he will probably resort to his dictionary rather more often than would be necessary for an English reader of roughly similar educational level, while not allowing himself to be disheartened by the thought that a whole wealth of meaning lies hopelessly locked away from him unless he proceeds at the rate of four pages an hour.

The English language is in the same position as 'background' knowledge. A very great deal of such knowledge is acquired, like knowledge of the language itself, once the early mechanics of learning are finished with, from the actual business of reading. Just as one learns the meaning of a word without using the dictionary, simply because of its repeated appearance in certain contexts, so one can often arrive at an understanding of initially puzzling social practices, modes of behaviour, emotional reactions, and so on, simply because the book has itself explained them. Hardy's *The Mayor of Casterbridge*, for example, will present a whole world that is in most ways different from anything the African reader has himself known. Quite apart from the more obvious unfamiliarity of the setting, characters in the novel will often behave in ways which surprise him, since he has not seen such behaviour in his own environment. But it is doubtful whether much can be gained by earnestly explaining to the reader that a young Englishwoman living in a country town (to take a random illustration) will think it a perfectly natural thing to go for a walk by herself in the outlying countryside. This, and many other things done by both men and women in the novel, may strike him as odd. The chances are, however, that by the time he has reached the middle of the book, he will be able to accept the oddities and unfamiliarities as natural parts of the context in which they occur. They will no longer disturb him, and he will be free to concentrate upon what is basically and centrally human and interesting in the novel.

That is the ideal condition to arrive at. To reach it, however, means once again establishing a proper balance. In this, the teacher has a great responsibility. He must be prepared to discuss with his students those matters relating to alien societies which they find puzzling. Usually this will mean little more than giving what we have called 'basic information'. The time at which it was customary to 'take tea' in the kind of society Jane Austen describes, is a case in point. No one, presumably, will take that to be a very serious obstacle to understanding. The developing relationship between Elizabeth Bennet and Mr Darcy, however, could be a more awkward proposition. It is here that particular tact is needed. What the teacher should, in effect, say, is something like this: 'You may find it difficult to imagine this going on in exactly the same way in your own society. But does this really matter? Here are two human beings, placed in circumstances that are almost as far removed from those of modern British society as they are from those of your own. Can you not see, however, that what really matters is that they *are* human beings, that they are striving to come together (like human beings in quite different circumstances elsewhere), and that striving to come together makes them discover themselves as they actually are, in both strength and weakness?'

While we are on the subject of *Pride and Prejudice*, it is perhaps worth pointing out that the very opening sentence of that novel may, at the present date, be more comprehensible to an African than to an English reader: 'It is a truth universally acknowledged, that a single man in possession of a good fortune must be in want of a wife'. There is, indeed, a constant give and take between books and readers belonging to different periods and societies. This is one of the things which keep literature alive.

At the beginning of this chapter we looked at a passage from the work of a Nigerian novelist. Our point was that it afforded an example, to the African reader, of a close relationship between literature and life. What of the European or American reader? Do environmental differences debar him from understanding not only that passage but the whole of *Things Fall Apart*? The question is absurd. While there is no doubt that *part* of what interests such a reader of Achebe will be the account of an alien and vanishing society, it is equally true that the permanent value of *Things Fall Apart* is far from parochial, and that what must fundamentally interest the non-African reader (and here we have something very like our proposition about *Pride and Prejudice*) is this: 'Here is the account of the breakdown of a way of life, a way of life that had existed for centuries. It was never exactly the way of life my people knew, even long ago, but the people involved in this story are human beings, just as my people were and are. My people have known changes of a rather similar kind in the last 200 years. I see changes going on about me every day. So the work of this Nigerian writer means something to me because in it I find the eternal story of change, for better and for worse, which again and again overtakes us all.'

Actually an English reader is likely to be impressed by specific similarities between the processes described by Achebe and the consequences of the Industrial Revolution in Britain. African de-tribalization and urbanization began as a result of colonialism, which in turn sprang from that industrial and commercial expansion that brought about the break-up of the old English agrarian society—a break-up chronicled, at different stages, by writers like Cobbett, Hardy, and George Sturt. And this suggests one reason why newly emergent countries have a positive gain to expect from reading literature. A writer such as Thomas Hardy may help them to understand what is happening to them, and can offer them different ways of looking at the process by hinting at various attitudes which might be adopted in coming to terms with it.

The African or Asian student of English literature will find things in it which interest precisely because of their strangeness, and so, despite what has just been said, will the non-African reader of *Things Fall Apart*. There is no need to feel disturbed about this, no need to feel that such interest is non-literary and thus in some way 'illegitimate'. It is an interest provided by the work of literature itself. To project oneself imaginatively into the world of other human beings, human beings who inhabit societies utterly distinct from one's own as far as the surface goes, is an experience of immense value. In the world of today we are all trying to know each other. It is indeed our only real hope for the future. And in this, literature is our inestimable friend and helper. It can teach us about one another; and yet, at the same time as instructing us about the incidental differences which divide us, it can show us that we are fundamentally one.

We have said so much about the effect of literature upon the individual reader that we must briefly deal with one more point before the end of this chapter—the 'moral' effect of literature. This is not really a difficult question. A simple distinction has to be made. On the one hand we have works of literature which quite definitely set out to demonstrate a moral truth, such as 'Pride goes before a fall'. Aesop's *Fables* are a famous example. More elaborate pieces of writing may have the same general kind of intention. We might take Samuel Johnson's poem *The Vanity of Human Wishes* as an instance. Johnson begins by proposing an overall view of the vain folly of humanity:

> Let observation with extensive view,
> Survey mankind from China to Peru;
> Remark each anxious toil, each eager strife,
> And watch the busy scenes of crowded life;
> Then say how hope and fear, desire and hate,
> O'erspread with snares the clouded maze of fate.
> Where wav'ring man, betray'd by vent'rous pride,
> To tread the dreary paths without a guide;
> As treach'rous phantoms in the mist delude,
> Shuns fancied ills, or chases airy good.
> How rarely reason guides the stubborn choice,
> Rules the bold hand, or prompts the suppliant voice.

After giving a series of illustrations of mankind's vanity, Johnson opens the last section of his poem as follows:

> Where then shall hope and fear their objects find?
> Must dull suspense corrupt the stagnant mind?
> Must helpless man, in ignorance sedate,
> Roll darkling down the torrent of his fate?
> Must no dislike alarm, no wishes rise,
> No cries invoke the mercies of the skies;
> Inquirer, cease, petitions yet remain,
> Which heaven may hear, nor deem religion vain.
> Still raise for good the supplicating voice,
> But leave to heaven the measure and the choice.

We may or may not actually profit from the lesson Johnson is giving us. It is probable that most of us will be aware of the superb vitality of his language ('Must dull suspense corrupt the stagnant mind?'), and that what we have in the poem is a tough and uncompromising mind focusing upon the eternal strangeness of humanity, even though we may not agree with its conclusions. But, whether we agree with them or not, the poem will, if it has impressed us at all, have had a certain 'moral' effect upon us. It may have done this by actual teaching. On the other hand, it may have done this simply by bringing us into contact with things people do, and particular ways of looking at these things.

Literature need not deliberately set out to teach in order to have a moral effect upon the reader, but it is certain that no intelligent reader will for long be impressed by or satisfied with a work which has no moral import. He will want what he reads to be *about* something, and will reasonably demand that he should gain some kind of profit from it, even though he may not be able to describe such profit in terms of lessons learnt or errors avoided. One reason why great works of literature *are* great is their moral stature. They offer the reader wisdom—wisdom presented usually in more subtle forms than overt preaching; wisdom embodied in the author's presentation of life as he has experienced it; wisdom embodied, in a great novel for instance, in the handling of character and incident, things in which the reader is made, by the writer's art, to feel actively involved, involved as he is when contemplating character and incident in his own life. Anything that modifies a reader's ideas and feelings about his own and other people's lives has a moral effect upon him. Most good literature has this kind of moral effect, and it is a dangerous mistake to try and find a cut-and-dried 'moral' in works which decidedly do not set out to preach. *Macbeth* has a high degree of moral interest, in that it tells us a great deal about some aspects of human life; but it would be ludicrous to tie it down to one particular moral intention, and say that Shakespeare wrote it to demonstrate the evils of ambition. The evils of ambition are abundantly evident in the play. They do not, however, account for even half its impact.

In any case, even quite a definite and straightforward moral lesson may be conveyed to the reader without overt preaching. The next chapter will attempt to show how this can be done, and will also serve as an introduction to both fiction and poetry, the subjects of the two main sections of this book.

3. A STORY IN VERSE

The Demon Lover

1 'O where have you been, my long, long love,
    This long seven years and mair?'[1]
    'O I'm come to seek my former vows
    Ye granted me before.'

2 'O hold your tongue of your former vows,
    For they will breed sad strife;
    O hold your tongue of your former vows,
    For I am become a wife.'

3 He turned him right and round about,
    And the tear blinded his ee:[2]
    'I wad[3] never hae[4] trodden on Irish ground,
    If it had not been for thee.

4 'I might hae had a king's daughter,
    Far, far beyond the sea;
    I might have had a king's daughter,
    Had it not been for love o' thee.'

5 'If ye might have had a king's daughter,
    Yersel[5] ye had to blame;
    Ye might have taken the king's daughter,
    For ye kend[6] that I was nane.[7]

6 'If I was to leave my husband dear,
    And my two babes also,
    O what have you to take me to,
    If with you I should go?'

7 'I hae seven ships upon the sea—
    The eighth brought me to land—
    With four-and-twenty bold mariners,
    And music on every hand.'

8 She has taken up her two little babes,
    Kissed them baith[8] cheek and chin:
    'O fair ye weel,[9] my ain[10] two babes,
    For I'll never see you again.'

9   She set her foot upon the ship,
      No mariners could she behold;
      But the sails were o' the taffetie,[11]
      And the masts o' the beaten gold.

10 She had not sailed a league, a league,
      A league but barely three,
      When dismal grew his countenance,
      And drumlie[12] grew his ee.

11 They had not sailed a league, a league,
      A league but barely three,
      Until she espied his cloven foot,
      And she wept right bitterlie.

12 'O hold your tongue of your weeping,' says he,
      'Of your weeping now let me be;
      I will shew you how the lilies grow
      On the banks of Italy.'

13 'O what hills are yon,[13] yon pleasant hills,
      That the sun shines sweetly on?'
      'O yon are the hills of heaven,' he said,
      'Where you will never win.'

14 'O whaten[14] a mountain is yon,' she said,
      'All so dreary wi[15] frost and snow?'
      'O yon is the mountain of hell,' he cried,
      'Where you and I will go.'

15 He strack[16] the tap-mast[17] wi his hand,
      The fore-mast wi his knee,
      And he brake that gallant ship in twain,
      And sank her in the sea.

GLOSSARY. [1] *mair:* more.   [2] *ee:* eye.   [3] *wad:* would.   [4] *hae:* have.
[5] *Yersel:* yourself.   [6] *kend:* knew.   [7] *nane:* none.   [8] *baith:* both.
[9] *weel:* well.   [10] *ain:* own.   [11] *taffetie:* taffeta.   [12] *drumlie:* dark.
[13] *yon:* yonder.   [14] *whaten:* what.   [15] *wi:* with.   [16] *strack:* struck.
[17] *tap-mast:* top-mast.

This poem is what we call a *ballad*. A ballad is a folk-song, and, in one way or another, it nearly always tells a story. Very often, though not invariably, the story will be concerned with violent and even horrifying incidents; and, as in *The Demon Lover*, the supernatural is frequently an ingredient.

47

A true ballad is meant to be *sung*, so we must remember that when we read the mere words of a ballad we are experiencing only part of its total effect. It is only when words and music are united that a ballad can really be taken in as a whole. It is worth trying to obtain a performance of *The Demon Lover* on a gramophone record, in order to see just how much is added by the music. But at the moment we must occupy our minds with the words alone, and it will probably be agreed that there is plenty to interest us in this ballad even when the music is left out.

A true ballad is anonymous. We cannot tell who originally wrote it. There are many poems, like Scott's *Proud Maisis* or Coleridge's *The Rime of the Ancient Mariner*, which imitate certain features of the ballad, but this does not qualify them for inclusion in any authentic ballad collection. The English and Scottish ballads, in common with folk-songs in other parts of the world, have been handed down through the ages mainly by word of mouth—or, as we say, by 'oral tradition'. Today we can read the words and often the music of ballads in various collections and anthologies, but the ballads in them had a very long history before such books were even thought of. The singers of one generation handed the ballads down to the singers of the next generation, and so on over the years and the centuries. And in the process of being handed down in this manner, the ballads have undergone changes and modifications, so that many of them exist in a variety of different versions.

This is not the place to go into the interesting question of how the ballads were originally composed. What we shall be concerned with here is the way in which the poem *works*. We shall try to determine exactly what it is that gives this poem its *life*.

Before we ask how a poem works, we must make sure that we have at least a fair idea of what it is about. *The Demon Lover* is simple in this respect, as it tells a straightforward though uncanny story. A woman meets a man with whom she had once been in love, and whom she had apparently promised to marry some seven years previously. When she tells him that she cannot marry him now because she is already the wife of somebody else, he becomes sorrowful and bitter, saying that if it had not been for his faithfulness to her he might have married a princess. Then the woman asks him what sort of life he would give her if she should after all leave her husband and children to go away with him. His reply shows him to be a rich man, and the prospect of riches and luxury makes the woman leave her family. But her lover's ship has not sailed far when a terrifying change comes over him. The woman realizes, to her horror, that she has abandoned her family to follow, not a human being, but a devil. The demon has tempted her, she has fallen, and at the end of the ballad she is carried off to hell.

Those are the bare facts of the story. It will probably be agreed, however, that those facts alone do not properly account for the effect of the poem. Let us therefore examine the poem in detail, looking closely at the way in which the story is presented. The ballad begins with a simple passage of dialogue between the woman and the man. Notice that we are given no *description* of these people. We simply hear their voices, as it were, and we have to pick up the necessary information about them from what they say. It is rather like a scene in a play, or, better still, a shot from a film. Indeed, in his book *The Ballads*, M. J. C. Hodgart draws a most useful parallel between the way in which many ballads work and a certain important aspect of film technique.

Everyone who has been to the cinema knows that some of the most exciting effects in a film are produced by the device of switching from one 'shot' to another. We may suddenly be switched from a shot of a group of people shown in full-length to a close-up of the face of one of them. Or we may be switched from one scene to a completely different one, with tremendous effect. This technique, which is called *montage*, is remarkably similar to devices used in a large number of ballads. We shall use this parallel between film and ballad in our discussion of *The Demon Lover*.

Let us say, then, that in the first two stanzas we are given a 'shot' of the man and woman together, in the course of which we learn

49

some basic facts about them and their relationship with one another. The woman is first to speak:

> 'O where have you been, my long, long love,
>   This long seven years and mair?'
> 'O I'm come to seek my former vows
>   Ye granted me before.'
>
> 'O hold your tongue of your former vows,
>   For they will breed sad strife;
> O hold your tongue of your former vows,
>   For I am become a wife.'

At the beginning of the third stanza the 'camera' focuses on the man. We see him turn away in sorrow and disappointment. Then comes a 'close-up' of the man's face, showing the actual tears of disappointment in his eyes. We may imagine this close-up to be held through the next two lines and through the whole of the fourth stanza, as the man tells the woman of the glorious marriage he might have made had it not been for love of her. In the fifth stanza we switch to a close-up of the woman, sustained right through to the end of stanza six:

> 'If ye might have had a king's daughter,
>   Yersel ye had to blame;
> Ye might have taken the king's daughter,
>   For ye kend that I was nane.
>
> 'If I was to leave my husband dear,
>   And my two babes also,
> O what have you to take me to,
>   If with you I should go?'

This particular close-up is most important, because something is happening to the woman, and we can imagine the expression of her face changing as a new idea comes into her head. In the fifth stanza she is rather saucily telling the man that he ought to have married the princess, since he knew perfectly well that she herself was nothing of the kind. In stanza six it is clear that the *idea* of leaving husband and children has actually occurred to her. Maybe she is at present only playing with the idea, and does not take the matter seriously.

The vital point, however, is that *the idea has entered her mind*. Temptation has already begun its work.

Perhaps the most effective example of montage in this poem comes after the man's reply. We are not told whether the woman was subjected to further temptations. Nor do we learn how long it took the man to succeed. The woman could have made up her mind to leave her family there and then. On the other hand, it might have taken days or even weeks of subtle persuasion. But that is all beside the point. What does concern us is the fact that she falls, and the fact that she falls through a love of wealth and luxury. It is for those things that she sells her soul. And how brilliantly this is conveyed by the quick succession of different 'shots'! First we have the man telling the woman about his riches:

> 'I hae seven ships upon the sea—
> The eighth brought me to land—
> With four-and-twenty bold mariners,
> And music on every hand.'

Then immediately afterwards we switch to something entirely different—a 'shot' of the woman bidding her children farewell:

> She has taken up her two little babes,
> Kissed them baith cheek and chin:
> 'O fair ye weel, my ain two babes,
> For I'll never see you again.'

We do not need anybody to tell us what happened in between the two stanzas. The man did his utmost to persuade the woman to go with him, and finally she yielded. No; anything like that would be lame and feeble, quite apart from being totally unnecessary. The fact that she has fallen is brought home to us *directly*, simply by the switch from one 'shot' to another.

This again is followed by a 'shot' utterly different from the previous one. We see the woman boarding her lover's ship. We observe her looking about in some surprise at the apparent absence of sailors:

> She set her foot upon the ship,
> No mariners could she behold;

Then surprise gives way to satisfaction as her eyes, and the 'camera', focus on the fabulous richness of the ship's rigging:

> But the sails were o' the taffetie,
> And the masts o' the beaten gold.

In the next stanza the ship is already at sea. First comes a close-up of the man's face, in which we, as well as the woman, are made to realize that a change is coming over him. And then the 'camera' frighteningly picks out that part of the man's body which shows him for what he is—the cloven foot of the devil. There remain three more main 'shots', with intermediate subsidiary ones of the devil and the woman talking. The first 'shot' is of the pleasant 'hills of heaven', the second brings before our eyes the grisly 'mountain of hell', and the last shows us the ship violently breaking up and sinking.

It will be noticed that there is absolutely no 'padding' in the presentation of this story. Nothing is put in that can possibly be left out. The story is pared down to the bare essentials. And what vividness and force are given to the narrative by this simplicity and directness, this absence of fuss and bother!

But there are still more things to be said about the poem, things which concern the way in which it communicates an imposing moral significance to the reader. Let us return to the ninth stanza:

> She set her foot upon the ship,
> No mariners could she behold;
> But the sails were o' the taffetie,
> And the masts o' the beaten gold.

There does not appear to be anything very remarkable about the simple second line of that stanza when we first read it. If we think for a moment about the line, however, we realize that, in an extremely direct way, it does have an immediate effect upon us. A person reading this poem for the first time, without having taken much notice of the title, would know as soon as he reached these words that there was something uncanny about the ship, and consequently something uncanny about her owner as well. We do not expect a ship to be apparently quite without men to sail her. Of course, all the sailors *might* conceivably at that moment be below deck. But this seems unlikely, and we are thus already inclined to suspect the presence of the supernatural. So the poem begins to build up an atmosphere of the weird and uncanny even before we learn the whole truth about the ship's owner in the next stanza but one. And this is done by the simplest of means.

But there is even more to be said about those same words, 'No mariners could she behold'. The woman is surprised, as we are, to find that there seem to be no sailors on board. Yet, we reflect, she may well be disconcerted for reasons which are different from ours. After all, the man for whom she has sacrificed her closest human ties has told her that the ship has 'four-and-twenty bold mariners'. (Obviously we are to assume that the ship which brought him to land is the one on which the woman is now embarking.) Let us try to imagine the reactions of this woman to the oddly deserted appearance of the ship. Can it be that the man has in some way deceived her? Can it be that she has left her family for a man less rich and prosperous than he claimed to be? But she is immediately reassured by the sight of the masts and sails:

> But the sails were o' the taffetie,
> And the masts o' the beaten gold.

A ship with rigging made of such materials clearly displays the wealth of her owner.

The words 'No mariners could she behold', in fact, tell us something about the woman's state of mind as she steps on board her lover's ship. Having abandoned her husband and children, she must feel guilty. And what could be worse than guilt arising from an action which has turned out not to have been worth while?

I have just said that the line *tells* us something about the woman's state of mind. But is this altogether correct? Is 'tells', indeed, the right word for what the line does? What the line actually *tells* us, what the line actually *states*, is merely the fact that the woman could see no mariners on board the ship. Yet, as we have seen, the line most

53

certainly does convey something to us about what the woman is thinking and feeling. No statement of any kind is made about her thoughts and emotions. We are left to infer what they may be. Her state of mind is *implied*.

There are other places in *The Demon Lover* where things are implied rather than stated. Take these stanzas, for example:

> 'I might hae had a king's daughter,
>   Far, far beyond the sea;
> I might have had a king's daughter,
>   Had it not been for love o' thee.'

> 'If ye might have had a king's daughter,
>   Yersel ye had to blame;
> Ye might have taken the king's daughter,
>   For ye kend that I was nane.

> 'If I was to leave my husband dear,
>   And my two babes also,
> O what have you to take me to,
>   If with you I should go?'

This demon is a subtle fellow, and he knows how most effectively to tempt the woman. He flatters her when he says that only his love for her prevented him from marrying a princess; but flattery is by no means his only weapon. His other reason for telling her this, a much more important reason, is implied by what follows. It is certainly no accident that the woman, after telling her 'long, long love' that he should have married the princess when he had the chance, and that it is not *her* fault if things have gone wrong for him, should take it into her head to ask him what prospects he holds out for her, just in case she did decide to leave her husband and children. We have seen already that she is a woman who adores money and luxury. Obviously such a woman would be quick to see that a man who 'might have had a king's daughter' must have an abundance of wealth behind him. So the demon lover is playing upon this weakness of hers, in addition to using straightforward flattery. Yet, once again, all this is *implied*, not *stated explicitly*.

54

Literature very often works by implying, as well as by stating explicitly. The line 'No mariners could she behold' explicitly states that the woman could see no sailors on board the ship. At the same time it implies something about her state of mind. We shall find some striking examples of this kind of technique when we come to examine passages from famous novels, in Chapter 4.

Now it may already have struck the reader that one extremely important thing in this ballad is implied, rather than stated explicitly: the moral significance of this strange tale. It was pointed out at the end of our last chapter that even quite a definite and straightforward moral lesson may be conveyed to the reader without overt preaching. *The Demon Lover* provides an excellent instance of this.

It is probable that no person, whatever his religious beliefs or disbeliefs, could be in two minds as to what we are expected to think of this woman. Clearly, she stands condemned. Admittedly she has been tempted; but she falls in the end, and the ballad seems to be telling us that her fate was a just and inevitable punishment for her weakness, wickedness, and folly. Yet it only *seems* to be telling us this. The ballad nowhere states explicitly that this is what we are meant to think. No formal 'moral' is drawn at the end, telling us to take heed and not fall into sin through vanity. Indeed, we cannot find the smallest explicit comment on the story, nor do we need such comment, so plainly does the moral significance emerge from the very way in which the story is told.

Consider, for example, the unfolding of the last five stanzas. When the woman discovers what kind of 'lover' she has eloped with, she weeps, partly out of fear, partly out of repentance:

> They had not sailed a league, a league,
> A league but barely three,
> Until she espied his cloven foot,
> And she wept right bitterlie.

But repentance has come too late. She is now firmly in the demon's clutches. She has fallen a victim to the lure of riches, and is already irrevocably damned. Her 'lover's' response to this sign of repentance is naturally one of impatience:

'O hold your tongue of your weeping,' says he,
'Of your weeping now let me be;

Impatience is followed by his old technique of holding out an alluring prospect:

I will shew you how the lilies grow
On the banks of Italy.'

This time the woman is not to be deceived. The 'banks of Italy' are ignored, for what she sees before her is something utterly different—a vivid pictorial representation of heaven and damnation:

'O what hills are yon, yon pleasant hills,
That the sun shines sweetly on?'
'O yon are the hills of heaven,' he said,
'Where you will never win.'

'O whaten a mountain is yon,' she said,
'All so dreary wi frost and snow?'
'O yon is the mountain of hell,' he cried,
'Where you and I will go.'

Notice the sudden impetus given by the word 'cried', as opposed to the previous 'says' or 'said'. It is a cry of triumph at the damnation of one more soul. From the violence of the demon's exclamation it is a short step to the violence of his actions in the last stanza:

He strack the tap-mast wi his hand,
The fore-mast wi his knee,
And he brake that gallant ship in twain,
And sank her in the sea.

When we remember that the masts he strikes are 'o' the beaten gold', a further significance emerges. It is for 'gold', amongst other things, that the woman has sold her soul. Yet with only two swift strokes, that richly adorned ship splits in two and sinks. The signs of wealth and luxury disappear into the depths of the ocean. 'All is vanity', the poem, once again, *seems* to be telling us. The gold and

56

the taffeta are gone. All that matters is that the woman has been carried off to eternal punishment.

Now, it would be absurdly untrue to say that all good literature communicates its deeper significance implicitly rather than explicitly. Samuel Johnson's *The Vanity of Human Wishes*, which we glanced at in Chapter 2, is an example of a fine poem which does nothing of the kind. In fact, its great strength is the power with which it *states*. Nevertheless, it is an odd fact in the experience of many readers, that something implied is often very much more effective, very much more powerful, than something stated explicitly. To explain this is not altogether easy. Probably the main reason is that more is required of the reader when something is being conveyed implicitly than when it is being explicitly stated. In the case of explicit statement, the reader is simply being told something, in a more or less straightforward way, and all he has to do is pay ordinary attention to what is being said. But to catch something which is implied demands a different kind of attention. It requires the reader actively to use his intelligence and imagination. The writer cannot do the whole job himself. If the reader does not use his intelligence and imagination to catch what is being implied, he will not properly understand what the writer has put down.

All this may sound rather contradictory. It may seem absurd to maintain that a way of saying something that demands *extra effort* from the reader is frequently more effective than explicit statement. It may seem that such a method of communication is likely to be less effective. Yet, curiously enough, this is not so. And at least part of the secret appears to be that when a writer implies something, and therefore demands additional effort from the reader, he is asking the reader for his active co-operation. He is, in a way, taking the reader into his confidence. It is as though he were saying to the reader: 'The success of what I have written now depends on you. I have done my part of the job. It is for you to complete the work for me.' Thus, when the reader co-operates with the writer by using his intelligence and imagination to catch what is being implied, he has a sense of personal involvement in the work he is reading. He experiences a feeling of being far more 'drawn into' the poem, play, or novel, than he would have been had it consisted merely of explicit statements. And, because of this added involvement, the effect of the work upon him is especially powerful and telling.

There is a further reason for the success of *The Demon Lover*. In most people there is a natural resistance to overt preaching in a work of literature, and in many other contexts as well. We have seen that this ballad, whether we are Christians and believe in heaven and damnation or not, contrives to present a moral lesson almost without letting the reader know that it is setting out to do anything of the kind. This has a great deal to do with the value of the poem, and also with the whole question of a work of literature and the beliefs, religious or otherwise, which lie behind it. Chapter 2 attempted to show that it is not necessary to share a writer's 'background' in order to grasp the human value of what he has to say. This is particularly true when the 'background', especially when it involves religious matters, is not made obtrusive to the reader. If *The Demon Lover* overtly preached that love of riches can all too easily lead to damnation, it would command the attention only of those who share the Christian assumptions implicit in the poem. As it is, those assumptions are only *implicit*. They are not obtrusive; and the reader who does not necessarily agree with them is not debarred from a work of art which can enlarge his understanding of human behaviour and moral codes.

PART II

4. THE NOVEL

What is it that interests us in a novel? The most obvious answer is 'the story'. But do we always know exactly what we mean when we talk about 'enjoying the story'? What precisely is it that we enjoy?

A story, we all know, is made up of a series of events, events arranged in such a way that there seems to be a natural rightness in the fact that the one comes just where it does after the other. This does not necessarily mean that we may not be intensely surprised, or even shocked, by 'the way things turn out'. Indeed, the capacity to surprise by some unlooked for twist in the narrative has for centuries been among the imaginative writer's most powerful resources. But, however defeated our expectations may be, however strongly we may feel that such-and-such a turn of events has not been 'fair' to the characters involved, we will always end by being convinced, when we read a good novel, that 'things *had* to be like that'.

There is an almost ridiculously simple reason why this should be so. It is common to say of a novelist that he 'tells a good story'. Yet not everyone who praises a writer in that way knows quite what he is praising him for. To say that a novelist tells a good story is, fundamentally, to record that one has been interested, stimulated, or excited, *by certain things that the writer has set down on paper.* This may seem stupidly elementary, but it is often forgotten. Admittedly, the novelist will probably first conceive his story, his 'plot', in terms which are quite independent of the words in which it will eventually be told to the reader. That does not matter. It only matters that the plot, whatever modifications it may have undergone in the writer's mind before the finished novel emerges, is conveyed to the reader because it has been cast into the form of

61

patterns of words which the reader sees before him on the page. The only idea that the reader can obtain of a novel's plot is the one he gains from the words in which the book is written. If this point seems obvious, it is worth recalling that reviewers of novels in newspapers and popular magazines frequently discuss them as though their plots, in some strange way, existed independently of their authors! Even if the novelist has indeed founded his plot closely upon something that has actually happened, as in the case of certain historical novels, the reader still has no way of getting at that plot except through the words the writer has used. The writer, if he is a good one, will thus always be in *complete control*. What happens in the novel (or play) cannot exist in some kind of peculiar territory removed from him. It is for this reason that a successful novel will leave us with the conviction, whatever doubts may from time to time have entered our minds, that 'things *had* to be like that'.

What we have said about 'plot' is true also of 'character'. And here we meet a further misconception regarding the novel, which still appears to be widespread even among those who write professionally about fiction—the notion that 'plot' (what happens in a novel) and 'character' (the people that the novelist is writing about) can be usefully discussed in separation from one another. 'The characters are well drawn, but the plot fails to convince'— that type of comment is depressingly common. I say 'depressingly' common, mainly because it so often turns up in school and undergraduate essays, and in answers to examination questions. One may find it convenient occasionally to concentrate upon some particular aspect of a novel. We shall be doing that very thing ourselves later in this chapter. But we must never allow ourselves to lose sight of the basic truth that *a novel is a whole*. Our examination of Wordsworth's *The Solitary Reaper*, in Chapter 2, showed that poem to be a very closely worked-out *whole*. A good novel is equally a *whole*. How can we talk about the plot of a novel without talking about its characters as well? How can we discuss what 'happens', in isolation from the people to whom it happens? If the plot of a novel 'fails to convince' it is likely that its characters are much less 'well drawn' than the critic imagines. Failure in one aspect of the book will reflect failure in another. Or it may (and often does) reflect the critic's failure to understand what the author is doing.

Reviewers of fiction in the popular press, not to mention the editors of many old-fashioned cheap editions of famous classics in fiction, may give a misleading impression of what we mean by 'character' in the novel. A book will be praised because its characters are 'lifelike', because 'we come to know them as though they were real people in our own lives'. So far there is nothing seriously to question in this. We have in a number of places already stressed the importance of realizing that an art which concerns itself with people must affect the way one leads one's own life. When the reviewer or editor goes on, however, to speak of a novel's characters as though they had some kind of existence outside the book, we are justified in feeling indignant. 'His characters are our lifelong friends. We continue to think about them, and imagine their future fortunes, after we have closed the book.' It is right that we should think about the characters in a novel, provided that we think about them *relevantly*. This means thinking about them *in relation to what the particular novel as a whole sets out to give us*, thinking about them *in connection with what the author has to say*. To think of them as being in any way independent of this, or to speculate on their 'future fortunes', is a waste of time, and has nothing to do with the experience offered to us by the book.

We shall have more to say about the general status of 'character' in the novel as we examine a series of passages introducing a selection of persons from Jane Austen, Hardy, George Eliot, and Dickens. Before we begin, there is a word of caution required. Just as we observed that 'the sole idea that the reader can obtain of a novel's plot is the one he gains from the words in which the book is written', so we must insist that the only way in which we can 'get to know' the characters in a novel is to pay attention to what the author has put down on the page. Our response to a personage in a novel is our response to certain words used by the author, words in which he describes the personage, words spoken by the personage himself, words spoken about him by other characters in the book, and so on. *Close acquaintance with an author's characters thus entails careful study of the way he uses language.*

With that in mind, let us commence our study of 'character' in four famous novels. The first passage comes from Jane Austen's *Pride and Prejudice.*

Mr. Bingley was good-looking and gentlemanlike; he had a pleasant countenance, and easy, unaffected manners. His sisters were fine women, with an air of decided fashion. His brother-in-law, Mr. Hurst, merely looked the gentleman; but his friend Mr. Darcy soon drew the attention of the room by his fine, tall person, handsome features, noble mien, and the report which was in general circulation within five minutes after his entrance, of his having ten thousand a-year. The gentlemen pronounced him to be a fine figure of a man, the ladies declared he was much handsomer than Mr. Bingley, and he was looked at with great admiration for about half the evening, till his manners gave a disgust which turned the tide of his popularity; for he was discovered to be proud; to be above his company and above being pleased; and not all his large estate in Derbyshire could then save him from having a most forbidding, disagreeable countenance, and being unworthy to be compared with his friend.

Mr. Bingley had soon made himself acquainted with all the principal people in the room; he was lively and unreserved, danced every dance, was angry that the ball closed so early, and talked of giving one himself at Netherfield. Such amiable qualities must speak for themselves. What a contrast between him and his friend! Mr. Darcy danced only once with Mrs. Hurst and once with Miss Bingley, declined being introduced to any other lady, and spent the rest of the evening in walking about the room, speaking occasionally to one of his own party. His character was decided. He was the proudest, most disagreeable man in the world, and everybody hoped that he would never come there again. Amongst the most violent against him was Mrs. Bennet, whose dislike of his general behaviour was sharpened into particular resentment by his having slighted one of her daughters.

On the surface, the passage seems to be giving a straightforward description of a group of people, with most of the attention devoted to Mr Bingley and Mr Darcy. The greater part of the description is done from the point of view of the other persons present at the ball. This becomes evident after the first few sentences, when we are made to focus on Mr Darcy. No particular point of view can be made out in the opening declaration that 'Mr. Bingley was good-looking and gentlemanlike'. As soon as Mr Darcy appears, however, we are conscious of seeing him as he is seen by the rest of the company in the room. We are not merely told that he had a 'fine, tall person, handsome features', and 'noble mien'. We are meant in addition to take notice of the fact that these things '*drew the attention of the room*'; these things, and also 'the report which was in general circulation within five minutes after his entrance, of his having ten thousand a-year'.

It is with the mention of this 'report' that the reader, if he is being vigilant, will begin to suspect that the passage is concerned with more than straightforward description. To be sure, the 'report' is left until *after* the reference to Mr Darcy's handsome physical attributes; but this does not mean that we therefore attach less importance to it than to them. The reverse is the case. Indeed, it is hard for us not to imagine this part of the passage rewritten as follows:

...but his friend Mr. Darcy soon drew the attention of the room by his fine, tall person, handsome features, noble mien, and (last, *but by no means least*) the report....

The 'report' does not merely communicate information about Mr Darcy; it also tells us something about the company in the room in general. When the writer goes on to say that

The gentlemen pronounced him to be a fine figure of a man, the ladies declared he was much handsomer than Mr. Bingley, and he was looked at with great admiration for about half the evening,

she is passing an implied comment on these ladies and gentlemen—the comment that they are mercenary-minded, and that their admiration for Mr Darcy has more to do with his wealth than with his good looks.

It is not long, however, before we perhaps begin to feel that we may have been unjust in judging too harshly the mercenary values of these people. After all, Mr Darcy's pride creates a general disgust which his wealth is powerless to dispel. We wonder whether the values of those who find him unpleasant can be quite so sordidly mercenary as we thought, when Jane Austen tells us that

...not all his large estate in Derbyshire could then save him from having a most forbidding, disagreeable countenance, and being unworthy to be compared with his friend.

Yet the matter is not as simple as that. Admittedly it is encouraging to find that considerations of social behaviour weigh more than considerations of property. But an implied judgment is still being made against these ladies and gentlemen at the ball, and it is the judgment *that they are fickle and superficial.* How else can one describe their ability to praise his looks to the skies for half the evening, and then to discover that he has 'a most forbidding, disagreeable countenance'? Granted that a person's behaviour may in time change the impressions one first had of him, there is still a sense of absurdity about the easy way in which these people can turn from one feeling towards Mr Darcy to its absolute opposite.

This is confirmed by what follows in the next paragraph. It becomes obvious that the standpoint from which these ladies and gentlemen judge a stranger is a purely *social* standpoint, in the most limiting sense of the word 'social'. Mr Bingley and Mr Darcy are seen and judged solely in accordance with the way they go through or fail to go through the motions regarded as proper to a social occasion such as a ball. Mr Bingley contrives to flatter the most prominent people in the assembly by going out of his way to acquaint himself with them. He is 'lively and unreserved', and an indefatigable dancer. What is more, by talking of giving a ball at Netherfield, he holds out a prospect of future social gratification for those lucky enough to be his guests. Charmed and delighted by his social gifts, the company make up their minds about him: 'Such amiable qualities must speak for themselves'.

They are equally assured about Mr Darcy, but in quite another direction: 'His character was decided. He was the proudest, most disagreeable man in the world, and everybody hoped that he would never come there again'. For this the reasons are not hard to find. Unlike his friend, he presents the appearance of being utterly uninterested in this kind of social function. He does not wish to make any new acquaintances, speaks only to members of his own party, and dances only twice. The reaction of the other guests is hardly to be wondered at: 'What a contrast between him and his friend!'

Now, it is true that Mr Darcy does not at this stage in the book make a very favourable impression upon the reader. The reader, indeed, may tend to sympathize with the ladies and gentlemen at the ball in their harsh criticisms of him. Certainly it is a long time before the central character of the novel, Elizabeth Bennet, comes to view him with any kind of liking. Pride and reserve are prominent in him; yet, as the novel eventually shows us, they are far from accounting for the whole man. He has an intelligence, an integrity, and a deep concern for the well-being of those to whom he is attached, which make him emerge as decidedly superior to his undeniably charming but not very interesting friend Bingley. And the possibility of this, the possibility that the company at the ball are undervaluing Darcy simply because he does not accord with their idea of 'amiable' social behaviour, is implied in the passage we are examining. If we are reading with real attention, we find ourselves doubting the wisdom of taking too much notice of what these ladies and gentlemen think of Mr Darcy. 'His character was decided'— decided for *them*, not for us. And the sheer exaggeration of the next sentence carries with it an implied comment on the superficiality of the people who could 'decide' such a thing so easily: 'He was the proudest, most disagreeable man *in the world*, and *everybody* hoped that he would never come there again'.

We may ourselves pass judgment on Mr Darcy, and say that he ought to have acted in a more 'amiable' manner at this social occasion. Mr Darcy does grow a great deal more 'amiable' as the book goes on, though his amiability reveals itself as a far deeper matter than the purely 'social' charm of his friend. Whatever doubts we may harbour about him at this stage, however, we should not allow ourselves to side uncritically with the other guests at the ball. If we sympathize with them in some ways, we should at the same time be as critical of them as we are of Mr Darcy. Although this is only Chapter 3 of *Pride and Prejudice*, we have read enough already to be convinced that Mrs Bennet is an exceptionally fatuous woman. The fact that she is 'among the most violent against him' should therefore put us on our guard against the judgment of the ladies and gentlemen at the assembly, and the values according to which they judge.

Detailed examination of what Jane Austen *says* in the passage, then, shows it to be more complicated and more interesting than we might at first have supposed. In it the novelist has contrived to do three things: (*a*) she has given us a few simple facts about a group of people, with Mr Bingley and his friend as the main focus; (*b*) she has implied a strongly critical feeling towards the company at the ball, and its values; and (*c*) by implying such an attitude towards the detractors of Mr Darcy, she has suggested that there is more to him than immediately meets the eye, and has thus pointed forward to later developments in the book.

Rather less subtle and concentrated, but in its own way equally interesting, is our second example, from *The Mayor of Casterbridge* by Thomas Hardy. A great banquet is taking place at the leading hotel of Casterbridge, with Michael Henchard, the mayor himself, in the chair. Unknown to him, his wife (or rather the woman who had once been his wife), and his daughter Elizabeth-Jane, are among a group of people out in the street looking through a window at the lively scene within:

Now the group outside the window had within the last few minutes been reinforced by new arrivals, some of them respectable shopkeepers and their assistants, who had come out for a whiff of air after putting up the shutters for the night; some of them of a lower class. Distinct from either there appeared a stranger—a young man of remarkably pleasant aspect— who carried in his hand a carpet-bag of the smart floral pattern prevalent in such articles at that time.

He was ruddy and of a fair countenance, bright-eyed, and slight in build. He might possibly have passed by without stopping at all, or at most for half a minute to glance in at the scene, had not his advent coincided with the discussion on corn and bread; in which event this history had never been enacted. But the subject seemed to arrest him, and he whispered some inquiries of the other bystanders, and remained listening.

When he heard Henchard's closing words, 'It can't be done', he smiled impulsively, drew out his pocket-book, and wrote down a few words by the aid of the light in the window. He tore out the leaf, folded and directed it, and seemed about to throw it in through the open sash upon the dining-table; but, on second thoughts, edged himself through the loiterers, till he reached the door of the hotel, where one of the waiters who had been serving inside was now idly leaning against the door-post.

'Give this to the Mayor at once,' he said, handing in his hasty note.

Elizabeth-Jane had seen his movements and heard the words, which attracted her both by their subject and their accent—a strange one for those parts. It was quaint and northerly.

The waiter took the note, while the young stranger continued—

'And can ye tell me of a respectable hotel that's a little more moderate than this?'

The waiter glanced indifferently up and down the street.

'They say the Three Mariners, just below here, is a very good place,' he languidly answered; 'but I have never stayed there myself.'

The Scotchman, as he seemed to be, thanked him, and strolled on in the direction of the Three Mariners aforesaid, apparently more concerned about the question of an inn than about the fate of his note, now that the momentary impulse of writing it was over. While he was disappearing slowly down the street the waiter left the door, and Elizabeth-Jane saw with some interest the note brought into the dining-room and handed to the Mayor.

Henchard looked at it carelessly, unfolded it with one hand, and glanced it through. Thereupon it was curious to note an unexpected effect. The nettled, clouded aspect which had held possession of his face since the subject of his corn-dealings had been broached, changed itself into one of arrested attention. He read the note slowly, and fell into thought, not moody, but fitfully intense, as that of a man who has been captured by an idea.

By this time toasts and speeches had given place to songs, the wheat subject being quite forgotten. Men were putting their heads together in twos and threes, telling good stories, with pantomimic laughter which reached convulsive grimace. Some were beginning to look as if they did not know how they had come there, what they had come for, or how they were going to get home again; and provisionally sat on with a dazed smile. Square-built men showed a tendency to become hunchbacks; men with a dignified presence lost it in a curious obliquity of figure, in which their features grew disarranged and one-sided; whilst the heads of a few who had dined with extreme thoroughness were somehow sinking into their shoulders, the corners of their mouth and eyes being bent upwards by the subsidence. Only Henchard did not conform to these flexuous changes; he remained stately and vertical, silently thinking.

As in the Jane Austen passage, the main interest here is centred on two characters, each of whom, as the book unfolds, will have far-reaching effects upon the other. The young man who at this point makes his first appearance in the novel will himself become Mayor of Casterbridge, as a result of the train of events started by his impulsive action. Henchard, on the other hand, who begins by conceiving an almost extravagant friendship for the young man, will sink into disaster and disgrace, and will come to look upon the young man as his bitter enemy.

You will have observed that the descriptions we are given of the aspect and actions of both Henchard and Farfrae (for that is the young man's name) are extremely simple and straightforward—so simple and straightforward, in fact, that you may consider that to comment on them would be superfluous. Beneath the simplicity, however, there is the grasp of the expert novelist, the control of the writer who sees this passage, like anything else in the book, as part of a carefully organized whole. Hardy does not bother to give a detailed account of Farfrae's physical appearance. He concentrates rather upon the instantaneous impression that Farfrae makes upon persons seeing him for the first time. He is concerned, indeed, with Farfrae's 'aspect', which is 'remarkably pleasant'. Only one short sentence of physical description is needed: 'He was ruddy and of a fair countenance, bright-eyed, and slight in build'. Hardy has an important reason for thus virtually paring down the description of Farfrae to the barest essentials. Farfrae's 'remarkably pleasant aspect' is one of the things which lead to his staying in Casterbridge and eventually becoming Mayor. It makes him easily liked and accepted; and, quite apart from his actual usefulness to Henchard, it has much to do with the Mayor's early fondness for him. Thus, by narrowing his description down to the immediate impression made by Farfrae's 'aspect', Hardy prepares the way for future events, events which have a good deal of connection with the young man's agreeable personality.

Farfrae's character is also revealed here in the things he does. In one way he resembles Henchard. Both are men of impulsive nature. But the resemblance does not go very far. Farfrae's impulsiveness, unlike Henchard's, does not get the better of him. It is controlled by another factor in his disposition—a vein of sober, cool reflection. And here, on Farfrae's very first appearance, the writer contrives to indicate at once the resemblance and the contrast between the two men. Henchard's impulsiveness has been abundantly revealed to us already in the astonishing first chapter of the book, where he sells his wife to a stranger in a bout of drunkenness. It will be revealed to us again in the way in which he decides to engage Farfrae to work for him. Here, by contrast, is Farfrae:

When he heard Henchard's closing words, 'It can't be done,' *he smiled impulsively*, drew out his pocket-book, and wrote down a few words by the aid of the light in the window. He tore out the leaf, folded and directed it, and seemed about to throw it in through the open sash upon the dining-table; but, *on second thoughts. . . .*

We cannot help setting this alongside something Hardy tells us about Henchard, after his reception of Farfrae's note: 'He read the note slowly, and fell into thought, not moody, but *fitfully intense*, as that of a man who has been *captured by an idea*'. Farfrae, too, has been 'captured by an idea'. How else can one describe his impulsive writing of the note? But Farfrae, though 'captured', is very plainly not the *slave* of his idea. Indeed, what we see of him once the note has been sent suggests that the idea means little to him:

The Scotchman...strolled on in the direction of the Three Mariners aforesaid, apparently more concerned about the question of an inn than about the fate of his note, now that the momentary impulse of writing it was over.

The predominant impression is that of a cool and, above all, self-possessed young man. When Henchard, on the other hand, is 'captured by an idea', we feel that he really *is* captured by it. Once it has a hold upon him, he cannot escape from it. Incident after incident in the novel will illustrate this trait in his make-up. Moreover, we would find it difficult, even at this stage of the book, to associate the words 'fitfully intense' with Farfrae. They certainly indicate the very opposite of coolness and self-possession.

Subordinate figures, appearing so briefly that they can hardly be called 'characters' at all, contribute to the notion we receive of the two men. Take the waiter to whom Farfrae gives the note. He is found 'idly leaning against the door-post', and when Farfrae asks him a question, he answers 'languidly'. Farfrae's energetic, active nature is made to stand out by contrast with the waiter's lethargy. Furthermore, Farfrae is not a man who minds putting a straight question, even though it involves revealing that he is not financially in a position to stay at the chief hotel in Casterbridge. Once again this is emphasized by means of contrast. Farfrae's question is absolutely forthright, whereas the waiter can scarcely bring himself to discuss the possibility of there being another hotel in the town. He glances 'indifferently up and down the street' to show his utter lack of interest in the matter, and his feeling of vast superiority to anyone who can contemplate lodging at an inferior hotel; and finally condescends to mention the name of one—though his words '*They say* the Three Mariners, just below here, is a very good place' tell us pretty clearly that he wishes to seem completely detached from the whole business. His parting shot, 'but I have never stayed there myself', reinforces this. He does not wish to be associated with the 'They' who speak well of the Three Mariners; and he tries to imply that *he*, were he in search of a room in Casterbridge, would certainly go to the King's Arms, the chief hotel itself! He is a snob, even though he is a menial. But Farfrae is not put out by this. He is concerned with only one thing—the question of somewhere to spend the night. Having obtained the information he wanted, he thanks the man, and goes on his own single-minded way, quite unperturbed by the waiter's insolence.

Henchard, too, is high-lighted by the use of contrast. He stands out in impressive isolation from the rest of the gathering. While other men put 'their heads together, in twos and threes, telling good stories with pantomimic laughter which reached convulsive grimace', Henchard remains 'stately and vertical, silently thinking'. The words 'stately and vertical' suggest an almost monumental quality in Henchard, appropriate to the central figure of what is to be a tragic story. And, when we look back at this passage from the closing pages of the novel, we realize that the pitiful isolation into which Henchard falls as his fortunes decline is here already foreshadowed.

The extreme plainness of Hardy's descriptions, then, must not deceive us into supposing that they are concerned only with the surface of things. Every point made in this passage goes home, and plays its part in the organization of the whole book. The same can be said of our next example, though one would scarcely think of calling it 'plain' in the same sense:

In a rather ill-favoured and ill-savoured neighbourhood, though one of its rising grounds bears the name of Mount Pleasant, the Elfin Smallweed, christened Bartholomew, and known on the domestic hearth as Bart, passes that limited portion of his time on which the office and its contingencies have no claim. He dwells in a little narrow street, always solitary, shady, and sad, closely bricked in on all sides like a tomb, but where there yet lingers the stump of an old forest tree, whose flavour is about as fresh and natural as the Smallweed smack of youth.

There has been only one child in the Smallweed family for several generations. Little old men and women there have been, but no child,

73

until Mr. Smallweed's grandmother, now living, became weak in her intellect, and fell (for the first time) into a childish state. With such infantine graces as a total want of observation, memory, understanding and interest, and an eternal disposition to fall asleep over the fire and into it, Mr. Smallweed's grandmother has undoubtedly brightened the family.

Mr. Smallweed's grandfather is likewise of the party. He is in a helpless condition as to his lower, and nearly so as to his upper limbs; but his mind is unimpaired. It holds, as well as it ever held, the first four rules of arithmetic, and a certain small collection of the hardest facts. In respect of ideality, reverence, wonder, and other such phrenological attributes, it is no worse off than it used to be. Everything that Mr. Smallweed's grandfather ever put away in his mind was a grub at first, and is a grub at last. In all his life he has never bred a single butterfly.

The father of this pleasant grandfather, of the neighbourhood of Mount Pleasant, was a horny-skinned, two-legged, money-getting species of spider, who spun webs to catch unwary flies, and retired into holes until they were entrapped. The name of this old pagan's God was Compound Interest. He lived for it, married it, died of it. Meeting with a heavy loss in an honest little enterprise in which all the loss was intended to have been on the other side, he broke something—something necessary to his existence; therefore it couldn't have been his heart—and made an end of his career.

This passage comes from *Bleak House*, by Charles Dickens. Probably the first thing that the reader will observe is that it is much more *elaborate* than our previous two examples. Indeed, it may initially seem that too many words are being used for a relatively simple matter. Why, for instance, should Dickens spend such a deal of time and language on Mr Smallweed's grandmother? What is the point of his telling us that 'There has been only one child in the Smallweed family for several generations'? We know perfectly well that this statement is literally untrue. Is the writer merely playing with us, trying to spin out somewhat thin material with a great flood of words?

Now Dickens has had, and doubtless always will have, his hostile critics; but before the reader decides to align himself with them, he would do well to consider what it is that the novelist is here setting out to do. Obviously Dickens is not at this stage interested in the

74

physical appearance of any member of the Smallweed family. What does concern him is a certain kind of *atmosphere* that surrounds all of them. This atmosphere is suggested in the very first words of the passage: 'In a rather *ill-favoured and ill-savoured* [i.e. ugly and smelly] neighbourhood...'. The predominant impression made by the Smallweed family as a whole is reflected in the locality in which they live. This parallel is taken further in the description of the 'little *narrow* street, always *solitary, shady, and sad, closely bricked in* on all sides *like a tomb*'. What immediately strikes us here is a sense of depression, a depression arising from the feeling of constriction associated with the street. It is as though the Smallweeds voluntarily pass their lives in a kind of prison. But that is not all. The street has a curious and interesting feature, 'the stump of an old forest tree, whose flavour is about as fresh and natural as the Smallweed smack of youth'. If this is a surprising object to find in such a neighbourhood, Dickens has put it there for a good reason. What this reason is will be apparent if we think for a moment about the name of this family—*Smallweed*. 'Weeds' they certainly are, as the rest of the passage, not to mention the rest of the book, amply demonstrates. Just as weeds strangle the growth of healthy plants, so this family exists by fastening upon unwary and unfortunate humans, and squeezing them dry. They are, in fact, parasites upon such people as walk into their trap. The 'stump of an old forest tree', then, makes us think of healthy growth stultified and blighted by a proliferation of malignant parasites: an army of 'weeds' none the less formidable for being 'small'.

There is more to be said about this tree-stump. Dickens tells us that its 'flavour is about as fresh and natural as the Smallweed smack of youth'. That is to say, its flavour, like that of the neighbourhood in general, is not fresh and natural at all. It smells of age and decay. '*Un*natural', indeed, is a word that immediately occurs to us in connection with the Smallweeds. They seem barely human, so preoccupied are they with the business of swindling and extortion. This characteristic of the family is so pronounced that it extends even to the children. The writer does not of course literally *mean* that there really have been no children in the family 'for several generations'. What he wishes to convey to us is that Smallweed children are utterly *unchildlike*, '*Little old men and women*', unnatural creatures old from birth, with the sordid mercenary character of their family stamped upon them in the very cradle. Mr Smallweed's grandmother, merely because she is old enough to have fallen into her dotage, is the first member of this squalid line to show any signs of being 'childlike'; yet the evidence of this is as completely unattractive as everything else about the family: 'such infantine graces as a total want of observation, memory, understanding and interest'. It is not to be wondered at that Dickens uses the word 'child*ish*' rather than 'childlike' to describe her condition. If she has, in a sense, become a 'child' in her old age, she is very far indeed from being a captivating one.

Mr Smallweed's grandfather, though physically almost completely paralysed, is mentally her opposite; but the words 'his mind is unimpaired' are not put there to awaken any admiration for him. If they should tempt us for one moment to be doubtful of the author's feelings towards him, the next two sentences make things perfectly clear: 'It holds, as well as it ever held, the first four rules of arithmetic, and a certain small collection of the hardest facts. In respect of ideality, reverence, wonder, and other such phrenological attributes, it is no worse off than it used to be.' He is, indeed, a fitting son for his father, that 'horny-skinned, two-legged, money-getting species of spider, who spun webs to catch unwary flies, and retired into holes until they were entrapped'. This gentleman sums up the overall impression we receive of the family: 'The name of this old pagan's God was Compound Interest. He lived for it, married it, died of it.' The very nature of his eventual fate is typical. He cannot be said to have died of a broken *heart*, since he showed no sign of ever having had one.

Our discussion of this passage should be looked at again after the later chapters on poetry. But one important point can be made now.

If the writing strikes us as being more elaborate than that of Jane Austen or Hardy, it is because Dickens makes extensive use of figures of speech. A great deal of the effect of the passage depends upon them. Take the *simile* in the first paragraph, so superbly conveying to us the atmosphere surrounding this repulsive family— 'a little narrow street, always *solitary*, *shady*, and *sad*, closely bricked in on all sides *like a tomb*'. Or consider the *metaphor* in which the grandfather is characterized: 'Everything that Mr. Smallweed's grandfather ever put away in his mind *was a grub at first, and is a grub at last. In all his life he has never bred a single butterfly.*' That is not merely an elaborate way of saying that his thoughts and feelings are base and contemptible. It links up with what is said about great-grandfather Smallweed in the next sentence. Both of these Smallweeds, father and son, are associated with particularly unattractive insects, and this helps to build up the overall feeling of revulsion with which we contemplate the family as a whole. The whole atmosphere of association with tombs, and decayed tree-stumps and holes in the ground, is linked to the reference to grubs and spiders.

One other feature of the passage must be mentioned before we pass on to the fourth example, and that is its *irony*. 'Irony' is a difficult word to define satisfactorily in general terms. Probably all that can really be said about it with any safety is that it always involves a sense of the incongruous. Two or more things are made to fit together, although we know full well that they can never genuinely fit. An obvious case of such incongruity in the present passage is great-grandfather Smallweed's 'honest little enterprise in which all the loss was intended to have been on the other side'. We can see perfectly clearly that when Dickens calls the enterprise 'honest', he means the exact opposite. There is a similar incongruity in the very name of the Smallweeds' neighbourhood—Mount Pleasant. It is impossible, by any stretch of the imagination, to connect the word 'pleasant' with this 'ill-favoured and ill-savoured' place. And can we really suppose that the dotage of Mr Smallweed's grandmother has 'undoubtedly brightened the family'? Could such a family ever be 'brightened' by anything, apart from the misfortunes of its victims?

Irony, of course, can be much more complex than this; but what Dickens does here is enough for his purpose. Just as Hardy throws the figures of Henchard and Farfrae into relief by means of contrast, so Dickens uses irony to intensify the disgust which the Smallweeds arouse in us. It is not easy, indeed, to think of a passage from any novel in which our sense of the characters described is more dependent upon close attention to the words the writer employs.

We shall conclude our discussion of the way in which a novelist presents character with an extract from George Eliot's *The Mill on the Floss*. Here are Mr and Mrs Glegg, uncle and aunt of Tom and Maggie Tulliver, the two central figures of the book:

Mrs. Glegg had both a front and a back parlour in her excellent house at St. Ogg's, so that she had two points of view from which she could observe the weaknesses of her fellow-beings, and reinforce her thankfulness for her own exceptional strength of mind. From her front windows she could look down the Tofton Road, leading out of St. Ogg's, and note the growing tendency to 'gadding about' in the wives of men not retired from business, together with a practice of wearing woven cotton stockings, which opened a dreary prospect for the coming generation; and from her back windows she could look down the pleasant garden and orchard which stretched to the river, and observe the folly of Mr. Glegg in spending his time among 'them flowers and vegetables.' For Mr. Glegg, having retired from active business as a woolstapler, for the purpose of enjoying himself through the rest of his life, had found this last occupation so much more severe than his business, that he had been driven into amateur hard labour as a dissipation, and habitually relaxed by doing the work of two gardeners. The economising of a gardener's wages might perhaps have induced Mrs. Glegg to wink at this folly, if it were possible for a healthy female mind even to simulate respect for a husband's hobby. But it is well known that this conjugal complacency belongs only to the weaker portion of the sex, who are scarcely alive to the responsibilities of a wife as a constituted check on her husband's pleasures, which are hardly ever of a rational or commendable kind.

The reader may immediately object, and with justice, that it is incorrect to claim that the passage really concerns itself with both

Mrs *and* Mr Glegg. Mr Glegg's appearance in this context hardly counts as a description of that gentleman himself. Instead, its function is to serve as one means of defining the character of his wife. What are we actually intended to think of Mrs Glegg? It is not quite so easy to answer that question as it would be to say what we are intended to think of the Smallweeds. If Dickens arouses in us exceedingly strong and positive feelings of antipathy, George Eliot is altogether more restrained, quieter, and more subtle. There is irony in this passage too; but it is less obvious and more cunning, at any rate until we reach the final sentence.

The best clue to George Eliot's intentions comes, conveniently, very soon after the opening: 'Mrs. Glegg had both a front and a back parlour in her excellent house at St. Ogg's, so that she had two points of view from which she could observe the weaknesses of her fellow-beings, and *reinforce her thankfulness for her own exceptional strength of mind*'. How seriously are we supposed to take this 'exceptional strength of mind'? Are we to accept it at its face value, and thus to regard Mrs Glegg as an admirable and unimpeachable woman? In other words, is the author really telling us, as a third party, that Mrs Glegg *had* 'exceptional strength of mind'? The answer is that George Eliot is recording Mrs Glegg's own flattering opinion of herself. This 'exceptional strength of mind' is simply a quality with which she has endowed herself, and for which she is perpetually thankful. And if we want evidence to support this view, we have only to consider her unamiable habit of observing the 'weaknesses of her fellow-beings' in order to bolster-up her own self-esteem.

The kind of 'weakness' she observes in her fellow-creatures hardly leads the reader to agree with her estimate of herself. In the outside world viewed from the windows of her front parlour, the sins of humanity amount to nothing more than a liking for going out on the part of certain other women (she calls it 'gadding about', and thinks that they ought to remain at home, as she does), and a partiality among them for woven cotton stockings (presumably a contemporary fashion which she obviously considers vain and

79

degenerate). As for the domestic prospect, scanned from the back parlour, it offers to her gaze nothing more terrible than the spectacle of her husband at his gardening. But even this adds fuel to the fire of her self-esteem, so convinced is she that what her husband does *must* be wrong, simply because her husband does it! Nothing will shake her conviction, not even the material consideration that Mr Glegg's labours save the expense of employing a gardener. It is not 'possible for a healthy female mind even to simulate respect for a husband's hobby'. Once again what we have here is Mrs Glegg's view of herself. The application of the adjective 'healthy' to her mind is her own, not George Eliot's. In the last sentence of the passage the irony is almost as broad as that of Dickens: 'But it is well known that this conjugal complacency belongs only to the weaker portion of the sex, who are scarcely alive to the responsibilities of a wife as a constituted check on her husband's pleasures, which are hardly ever of a rational or commendable kind'. 'The weaker portion of the sex' (i.e. the female sex) can be taken about as seriously as great-grandfather Smallweed's 'honest little enterprise'. Mrs Glegg very decidedly considers herself as belonging to the *stronger* portion of the sex, the portion which feels, as she does, that it is one of a wife's duties to criticize and curtail anything her husband happens to enjoy, however innocent it may be. The 'conjugal complacency' of attempting to 'simulate respect for a husband's hobby' is possible only to those weaker females who, unlike the self-righteous and self-congratulating Mrs Glegg, are too feeble-minded to be aware of their obligation to carp and dominate. If this is 'well known', it is 'well known' only to Mrs Glegg and her like.

One more point may be made about this passage. It will be observed that Mrs Glegg's circumstances are remarkably easy. She has 'both a front and a back parlour'; her house is described as 'excellent'; and at the back of it there are a 'pleasant garden and orchard' stretching to the river. Little wonder that, in such agreeable and comfortable surroundings, she might be given to self-congratulation on her good fortune. But this is by no means the bent of her mind. She plainly accepts these amenities as a matter of course. Esteeming herself as a woman of 'exceptional strength of mind', she obviously thinks that she deserves such comforts in any case; and, as for the husband who has contributed to them, she regards him merely as an object upon which to exercise her 'responsibilities'. And we cannot help reflecting that it is precisely the easiness of her circumstances that has given her the leisure to 'reinforce her thankfulness for her own exceptional strength of mind'.

Our four examples from famous novels should have made it apparent that we must read closely, with real attention to the words a writer uses, if we are to have any proper sense of the characters he or she is presenting. 'Character', however, is only one of the ingredients of a novel. What we must now look at is the way in which all the elements of fiction, the characters, the action, and the setting in which the action takes place, can be welded together into a tightly organized whole. To do this, we shall return to *The Mayor of Casterbridge*, though this time our concern will be with the actual opening chapter of the novel, the chapter which contains the astonishing incident of the sale of Henchard's wife. Let us try to see exactly what it is that Hardy is doing. Let us try to determine exactly the function of the things to which he draws our attention.

The first two sentences of the novel may not, in themselves, appear to offer much opportunity for comment. On the face of things, indeed, they seem to be imparting information, and nothing more:

One evening of late summer, before the nineteenth century had reached one-third of its span, a young man and woman, the latter carrying a child, were approaching the large village of Weydon-Priors, in Upper Wessex, on foot. They were plainly but not ill clad, though the thick hoar of dust which had accumulated on their shoes and garments from an obviously long journey lent a disadvantageous shabbiness to their appearance just now.

Yet there *is* more to this than plain information. The 'dust' and the 'shabbiness' resulting from it are not put there by Hardy merely to tell us about the condition of these people's shoes and clothing. They do have that function, to be sure; but, as we shall see, they are also connected with the prevailing atmosphere of the entire chapter, the atmosphere in which the central episode is enacted.

There follows a description of the man, in whom we are immediately made to sense something out of the ordinary:

The man was of fine figure, swarthy, and stern in aspect; and he showed in profile a facial angle so slightly inclined as to be almost perpendicular.... His measured, springless walk was the walk of the skilled countryman as distinct from the desultory shamble of the general labourer; while in the turn and plant of each foot there was, further, a dogged and cynical indifference, personal to himself, showing its presence even in the regularly interchanging fustian folds, now in the left leg, now in the right, as he paced along.

The man with this stern aspect, with this 'facial angle so slightly inclined as to be almost perpendicular', is to become the man we met in our earlier passage from this novel; the man who, amidst the jocular aftermath of the great ceremonial dinner, remains 'stately and vertical, silently thinking'. Something of his future monumental quality, the quality of a great tragic figure, is thus already suggested on his very first appearance. As for the 'dogged and cynical indifference, personal to himself', we shall soon be given proof of this in his behaviour as the chapter proceeds. But that is not all. 'Dogged' is a word which can be applied to Henchard throughout the whole book. If it has much to do with his strength, it has far more to do with his weakness; and, with a persisting strain of 'indifference' showing itself in a disastrous lack of tact in dealing with other men, it will eventually bring about his downfall.

One especially interesting feature of this opening chapter is that Hardy inserts an entire paragraph between the description of Henchard and that of his wife. He has a good reason for doing this, which will quickly be apparent to us from the substance of the paragraph:

What was really peculiar, however, in this couple's progress, and would have attracted the attention of any casual observer otherwise disposed to overlook them, was the perfect silence they preserved. They walked side by side in such a way as to suggest afar off the low, easy, confidential chat of people full of reciprocity; but on closer view it could be discerned that the man was reading, or pretending to read, a ballad sheet which he kept before his eyes with some difficulty by the hand that was passed through the basket strap. Whether this apparent cause were the real cause, or whether it were an assumed one to escape an intercourse that could have been irksome to him, nobody but himself could have said precisely; but his taciturnity was unbroken, and the woman enjoyed no society whatever from his presence. Virtually she walked the highway alone, save for the child she bore....

By deferring his description of the woman until after this account of the extraordinary manner in which they appear to be both together and separate at one and the same time, the author contrives *to emphasize the division between them.* Just as the paragraph separates the descriptions of the two people, so the absolute silence prevailing between them makes each one seem a separate and solitary figure.

What we are now told about the woman, though she is far less arresting than the man, has its own significance in the overall pattern:

The chief—almost the only—attraction of the young woman's face was its mobility. When she looked down sideways to the girl she became pretty, and even handsome, particularly that in the action her features caught slantwise the rays of the strongly coloured sun, which made transparencies of her eyelids and nostrils, and set fire on her lips. When she plodded on in the shade of the hedge, silently thinking, she had the hard, half-apathetic expression of one who deems anything possible at the hands of Time and Chance, except, perhaps, fair play. The first phase was the work of Nature, the second probably of civilization.

The subtle attractiveness of the young woman links up with what is to become of her only a few pages later. On the one hand we shall find Henchard, who does not appreciate her qualities, rejecting her in bitterness and derision. On the other hand there will be quite opposite reactions to her from other people who are able to perceive her unostentatious charm—like the comment of the man who says

'I've had my breedings in as good circles, I may say, as any man...
and I know true cultivation, or nobody do; and I can declare she's
got it—in the bone, mind ye, I say—as much as any female in the
fair—though it may want a little bringing out'. That may not be
a particularly elegant way of expressing praise, but the honest
appreciation it shows is very different from the attitude of her
husband. The 'hard, half-apathetic expression' worn by the woman's
face when she plods on 'in the shade of the hedge' will soon be
explained to us only too clearly. If she thinks that anything may be
possible except 'fair play', her husband's subsequent behaviour will
make us realize the kind of thing she has had to put up with in her
life with him, and will account for her gloomy acceptance of living
as a tissue of unfairness and misfortune.

We have been referring to the couple as husband and wife, which
indeed they are. The author, however, does not actually tell us that
this is their relationship until after the description of the woman.
Then comes this short, telling paragraph of two sentences:

That the man and woman were husband and wife, and the parents of the
girl in arms, there could be little doubt. No other than such relationship
would have accounted for the atmosphere of stale familiarity which the
trio carried along with them like a nimbus as they moved down the
road.

'Stale' is an important word here. Not only does it describe the
relationship between these two people; it also characterizes the
whole atmosphere of this part of the chapter. The very landscape
through which they are plodding has a 'stale' flavour. Uninteresting,
lacking in any pronounced features, it is a scene 'that might have
been matched at almost any spot in any county in England at this
time of the year; a road neither straight nor crooked, neither level
nor hilly...'. And over it all hangs the prevailing dust, the same
dust which powders the shoes and garments of the pedestrian
couple, imparting to the whole countryside, as well as to them, a
general air of 'shabbiness'. Even the silence enveloping the pair is
broken only by 'the voice of a *weak bird* singing a *trite old evening*

84

song that might doubtless have been heard on the hill at the same hour, and with the self-same trills, quavers, and breves, at any sunset of that season for centuries untold'.

The atmosphere of stale depression is intensified by the answers given to Henchard's questions by a labourer they meet on the road. When Henchard asks him if there is any work to be had in the village they are approaching, he replies with a shake of the head, and a question of his own:

'Why, save the man, what wisdom's in him that 'a should come to Weydon for a job of that sort this time o' year?'

'Then is there any house to let—a little small new cottage just a builded, or such like?' asked the other.

The pessimist still maintained a negative. 'Pulling down is more the nater of Weydon. There were five houses cleared away last year, and three this; and the volk nowhere to go—no, not so much as a thatched hurdle; that's the way o' Weydon-Priors.'

The hay-trusser, which he obviously was, nodded with some superciliousness. Looking towards the village, he continued, 'There is something going on here, however, is there not?'

'Ay. 'Tis Fair Day. Though what you hear now is little more than the clatter and scurry of getting away the money o' children and fools, for the real business is done earlier than this. I've been working within sound o't all day, but I didn't go up—not I. 'Twas no business of mine.'

In spite of the fact that the buying and selling of animals, which has been the 'real business' of the Fair, is now over, the crowd on the Fair-field is dense, intent on the various amusements offered by wandering entertainers. What Henchard and his wife, however, are looking for, is a refreshment tent, where they may restore their energies after their long weary walk. Two tents offer themselves, one of them selling a concoction called furmity, a 'mixture of corn in the grain, flour, milk, raisins, currants, and what not'. To this tent they betake themselves, at the wife's suggestion, and order a basin each of the steaming hot furmity. But, as Hardy points out, there is 'more in that tent than met the cursory glance'. It soon becomes plain that the woman who is making and selling the mixture, a 'haggish creature of about fifty', is engaged in a sly trade.

With the exchange of a nod and a wink, and the passing of the furmity basin up to her, she laces the concoction with rum, secretly kept below the table—an arrangement of which Henchard is quick to take advantage. He does not rest content with one basin, and the effects soon show themselves:

At the end of the first basin the man had risen to serenity; at the second he was jovial; at the third, argumentative; at the fourth, the qualities signified by the shape of his face, the occasional clench of his mouth, and the fiery spark of his dark eye, began to tell in his conduct; he was overbearing— even brilliantly quarrelsome.

The presence of the 'haggish creature', and the change overtaking Henchard, bring a new element into the atmosphere. The sense of stale depression is now deepened into a feeling of the positively sinister. We are certain that the man is likely to do something perverse, especially since Hardy has used the words 'with the instinct of a perverse character' to describe the way in which Henchard so quickly observes the 'haggish creature's' sly proceedings. The turn of the conversation gives him the cue for a display of his true nature. As the company in the tent bemoan 'The ruin of good men by bad wives, and, more particularly, the frustration of many a promising youth's high aims and hopes, and the extinction of his energies, by an early imprudent marriage', Henchard seizes upon the theme and enlarges upon its application to his own case: '"I married at eighteen, like the fool that I was; and this is the consequence o't." He pointed at himself and family with a wave of the hand intended to bring out the penuriousness of the exhibition.' His wife, however, does not appear at all perturbed by this. She seems 'accustomed to such remarks', and acts 'as if she did not hear them'. We begin to understand what it is that has given her that 'hard, half-apathetic expression'.

The voice of the auctioneer selling old horses, inferior animals not disposed of earlier in the day, in the field outside the tent, brings Henchard a new idea: 'For my part I don't see why men who have got wives, and don't want 'em, shouldn't get rid of 'em as those

86

gipsy fellows do their old horses....Why shouldn't they put 'em up and sell 'em by auction to men who are in want of such articles? Hey? Why, begad, I'd sell mine this minute if anybody would buy her!' No one is prepared to take this seriously as yet—at least, no one in the tent. The reader, however, remembers the 'dogged and cynical indifference' evident in the very way Henchard walks, and is thus made to fear that he will not be easily diverted from his theme. And indeed he is not. For a few seconds he pauses, wondering at the unlooked-for praise of his wife that we have already referred to, and which follows his blustering declaration. But he is not to be deflected from his course for long. On his return to the subject, his wife for the first time shows signs of concern. More of their past is revealed to us in her words, the past which has led her to expect anything save 'fair play': 'Michael, you have talked this nonsense in public places before. A joke is a joke, but you may make it once too often, mind!' Concerned though she obviously is, the woman tempers her warning with the tactful assumption that her husband does not, after all, really mean what he is saying. Her next words are uttered in a different tone, and with good reason. The people in the tent have been distracted from Henchard's offer of his wife by the entry of a bird through an opening in the upper part of the structure, all eyes absently following its flight to escape. This tiny incident, apparently so trivial, has an important function. For a quarter of an hour Henchard's subject is dropped, as a result of the distraction caused by the bird. Then, quite suddenly, he doggedly returns to it: 'Here—I am waiting to know about this offer of mine. The woman is no good to me. Who'll have her?' It is now easy to see why Hardy has introduced the seemingly unimportant little episode. It is brought in to leave us in no doubt as to the man's intentions. If he can hark back to a theme abandoned by the company for so long, he plainly must mean what he says, perverse and extraordinary though it is. Small wonder, then, that the woman's tone is now 'imploring and anxious'. She no longer even pretends to treat the matter as a joke: 'Come, come, it is getting dark, and this nonsense won't do. If you don't come along, I shall go without you. Come!' But the man does not move. Ten minutes pass, and his offer is renewed. This time there is a significant alteration in his wife's response:

> The woman's manner changed, and her face assumed the grim shape and colour of which mention has been made.
> 'Mike, Mike,' said she; 'this is getting serious. O!—too serious!'
> 'Will anybody buy her?' said the man.
> 'I wish somebody would,' said she firmly. 'Her present owner is not at all to her liking!'

For the company at large the affair is still a joke. A grotesque little man volunteers to act as auctioneer, while the woman stands before them, like a horse up for sale at the Fair. Yet the woman's very act of standing up, at her husband's command, shows that she, at last, is as much in earnest as he is. She has clearly had to take a great deal in the way of suffering from him already. Why, therefore, should she care what he chooses to do with her now? Thus, when Henchard fixes upon the sum of five guineas as the price for which he is prepared to part with her, she bows her head 'with absolute indifference'.

What everyone except the man, his wife, and the reader, regard as an excellent piece of fun, is at its height. The auctioneer lays down five guineas as the stipulated price of the woman. No one expects a seriously intended reply. Then comes the great dramatic stroke:

> 'Five guineas,' said the auctioneer, 'or she'll be withdrawn. Do anybody give it? The last time. Yes or no?'
> 'Yes,' said a loud voice from the doorway.
> All eyes were turned. Standing in the triangular opening which formed the door of the tent was a sailor, who, unobserved by the rest, had arrived there within the last two or three minutes. A dead silence followed his affirmation.

It is appropriate that he should first be seen standing in the door of the tent, apart from the rest of the company, not identifying himself with them, not sharing their notion that the whole proceeding is an uproarious entertainment. Upon Henchard's challenging him to show the money, the sailor advances into the tent, throws five pound notes down upon the table, and, on top of them, 'chinks' the shillings one by one—'one, two, three, four, five'. We must remember that there is otherwise a dead silence in the tent, so that the sound of the chinking shillings stands out with peculiar distinctness as a vividly audible sign that the sailor is in deadly earnest. And with this, the mood of the company changes. A sense of the perverse and the sinister seizes upon them at last:

Up to this moment it could not positively have been asserted that the man, in spite of his tantalizing declarations, was really in earnest. The spectators had indeed taken the proceedings throughout as a piece of mirthful irony carried to extremes; and had assumed that, being out of work, he was, as a consequence, out of temper with the world, and society, and his nearest kin. But with the demand and response of real cash the jovial frivolity of the scene departed. A lurid colour seemed to fill the tent, and change the aspect of all therein. The mirth-wrinkles left the listeners' faces, and they waited with parting lips.

There follows an exchange between the woman, her husband, and the sailor, in which Henchard, dogged as ever, remains utterly unrepentant. What is left for the woman to do but follow the man who shows more appreciation of herself and her feelings than her cynically indifferent husband? (The sailor has been careful to say ''Tis quite on the understanding that the young woman is willing.... I wouldn't hurt her feelings for the world.') But she has a parting shot in reserve. As she reaches the door of the tent, the opening in which the sailor has first been seen outlined, she pulls off her wedding-ring and throws it in her husband's face:

'Mike,' she said, 'I've lived with thee a couple of years, and had nothing but temper! Now I'm no more to 'ee; I'll try my luck elsewhere. 'Twill be better for me and Elizabeth-Jane, both. So good-bye!'
Seizing the sailor's arm with her right hand, and mounting the little girl on her left, she went out of the tent sobbing bitterly.

And so she disappears. The climax is over with astonishing speed. It is only a matter of minutes since the sailor's entry into the drama, framed in the opening through which he has vanished with Henchard's wife and child. Ironically enough—and here our sense of incongruity is extreme—she has gone away with the man who, after her two years of suffering with Henchard, has at last given her 'fair play'; 'fair play', however, at the price of a scandalous and illicit transaction! The author has told us, in describing the woman's face, that 'the hard, half-apathetic expression of one who deems anything possible at the hands of Time and Chance, except, perhaps, fair play' is probably the work of 'civilization'. How richly ironic it is, then, that she should know 'fair play' at the hands of a man who willingly engages in an act which is the very reverse of 'civilized', as the word is normally understood.

His wife gone, Henchard rises and walks to the door of the tent, followed by a few others who stand there 'looking into the twilight'. I commented near the beginning of this account that the prevailing atmosphere of the chapter is one of stale depression, with which the dustiness and shabbiness of the couple's appearance are associated. We have seen that stale depression take on a 'lurid colour', to use Hardy's own words. But now there comes a radical change, as we, together with the others who have followed Henchard to the opening, contemplate the serenity of the non-human world outside the tent in which the violent little drama has been performed:

The difference between the peacefulness of inferior nature and the wilful hostilities of mankind was very apparent at this place. In contrast with the harshness of the act just ended within the tent was the sight of several horses crossing their necks and rubbing each other lovingly as they waited in patience to be harnessed for the homeward journey. Outside the fair, in the valleys and woods, all was quiet. The sun had recently set, and the west heaven was hung with rosy cloud, which seemed permanent, yet slowly changed. To watch it was like looking at some grand feat of stagery from a darkened auditorium. In presence of this scene, after the other, there was a natural instinct to abjure man as the blot on an otherwise kindly universe; till it was remembered that all terrestrial conditions were intermittent, and that mankind might some night be innocently sleeping when these quiet objects were raging loud.

Hardy does not, you will observe, emphasize the tranquillity at the expense of truth. It may certainly be extremely tempting to 'abjure man as the blot on an otherwise kindly universe', when this scene is contrasted with that which has been enacted inside the tent. Yet to do this would be unpardonably *sentimental*. One of the most common forms of sentimentality is that which suppresses some aspect or aspects of a situation for the purpose of achieving a cheap and easy emotional effect. To ignore the fact that non-human nature is frequently anything but tranquil, while humanity quite commonly can be so, would be to fall into precisely that kind of trap. The contrast which he draws in the present context does not lead Hardy into any such pitfall, and is all the more telling for the realistic common sense with which it is qualified.

A novel, then, is a more complex affair than one would suppose from the glib way in which some critics of fiction parcel it up into 'plot' and 'character'. Fiction is a branch of literature. As such, it tells us what it sets out to say through the words the writer puts down on paper. Only through attention to what is *written*, therefore, can we hope to arrive at the author's whole meaning. Only through the words a novelist uses can a sense of his story, his characters, and his individual situations, be precipitated in our minds. Once we recognize this truth, seemingly so elementary yet so often ignored, we can safely proceed to consider, as we shall try to do in our next chapter, the ways in which these precipitates can be organized together on a large scale.

What we have concluded about fiction can be applied to the drama in prose. We all know that a play is meant for actual performance upon the stage, and that it does not truly come to life until it is acted. But that must not lead us to suppose that a good prose play, like *She Stoops to Conquer*, is a mere 'script', a mere collection of intrinsically lifeless dialogues and speeches which only the interpretative power of skilled actors and actresses can render tolerable. The life is already abundantly there in Goldsmith's handling of language, language intended to be spoken aloud on the stage, to be sure, but as carefully and consciously set down as anything in a good novel. Thus, before we start discussing such a character as Tony Lumpkin, let us establish firmly in our minds the truth that he, like everyone else in the play, *is fundamentally a product of language.*

5. SEEING A NOVEL AS A WHOLE

How should we read a novel? The obvious reply would seem to be that we begin at the beginning and go on to the end. It is certainly not suggested to the reader that he should start in the middle, and then ramble backwards and forwards until somehow the entire thing fits together. At least, such an approach is not recommended unless the reader knows the book extremely well, when it may on occasion be enlightening. Our preoccupation just now, however, is with the most efficient way of coming to terms with a good novel, and thus obtaining the maximum enjoyment and stimulus from it.

It can be said straight away that, for all but really experienced readers, a novel of the finer type will not reveal its full significance on the first reading. There is no need to be depressed about this. Even when a second reading has brought the reader more closely into touch with the book, there will remain new aspects of its meaning to emerge with each subsequent experience of it. However striking the initial impact of a fine work of art may be, its deeper significance is brought home to us in a *cumulative* way, developing over the years as we ourselves develop as human beings. It is nevertheless true that a deal of time and effort can be saved if the reader has some idea of what to look for when he approaches a novel for the first time.

Since every novel is an individual case, it would be folly to pretend that we can arrive at a formula of approach which can be simply applied to any example of the art of fiction that comes our way. One guiding principle may, however, be safely laid down: a novel, like any other work of literature, will have some central theme, some fundamental preoccupation, from which all discussion of the book must start. When the reader has recognized the nature of the writer's central concern, he will have found his own bearings, and

93

will thus be able to voyage through the book with a good idea of where his journey is taking him. Nothing can be more important for the teacher of literature than a firm grasp of a novel's basic preoccupation, since an initial knowledge of this is of inestimable help to his pupils. The student who is left to flounder through a novel with no adequate idea of what it is really all about, is rather pathetically wasting his time.

Let us take Jane Austen's *Pride and Prejudice* as an illustration. How ought we to approach this book? Are we to view it simply as a mildly amusing account of the way provincial English people in easy circumstances lived at that particular period in history? If that is so, how seriously are we expected to take the relationship between Mr Darcy and Elizabeth Bennet? The answer is that we are intended to regard that relationship as the very bedrock upon which the novel rests. *Pride and Prejudice* certainly entertains us with its picture of the manners and foibles of people like Mr Collins and Lady Catherine de Bourgh; but the essential thing to grasp is that these manners and foibles are significant precisely because they contribute to our understanding of the Darcy–Elizabeth Bennet relationship. Take the case of Mr Collins alone. He may seem at first to have no other function than to amuse us with his fatuity and to make some mechanical contributions to the advancement of the story. If we consider his marriage to Charlotte Lucas, however, we find that he has a more serious part to play than we had supposed. For Elizabeth Bennet there can be no question of marrying such a man. Her intelligence, her sense of fitness, and, not least, her sense of humour, cry out against the bare idea. Her friend Charlotte, on the other hand, while perfectly well aware of his demerits, accepts and marries him. Now, it is important to bear in mind that Charlotte Lucas is far from being a young woman of mean intelligence. If she were shown to us as being so, it would be impossible to imagine her as the close friend of Elizabeth Bennet. And yet she is capable of entering upon a lifetime of Mr Collins! What are we to say about her? The answer is provided by Charlotte Lucas herself, when Elizabeth incredulously questions her. She has no illusions about Mr Collins, but there are certain solid advantages in the match. With her eyes wide open to the situation, she accepts Mr Collins as a material proposition which it would be irrational and unrealistic to ignore. Elizabeth is shocked, despite her comprehension of Charlotte's motives. With a good share of reason and realism herself, she yet finds her friend's acceptance of Mr Collins fundamentally indefensible. To her it is something of a moral outrage that an intelligent woman, particularly one who has been her intimate friend, should descend to such a level. With the best will in the world, she cannot help protesting to Charlotte that her attitude towards the match is 'not sound'. And the result is that just as Charlotte Lucas, though never to be despised, somewhat disappoints us by her decision, Elizabeth Bennet very considerably gains in stature. Thus Mr Collins indirectly serves as one means of defining a valuable quality in Elizabeth, a quality which in fact counts for more than anything else in Mr Darcy's developing opinion of her. Both she and her friend Charlotte are young women of lively wit; but it is Elizabeth who blends wit with a degree of moral fineness and fastidiousness lacking in her ultra-realistic companion.

The Mill on the Floss becomes fully intelligible only when we realize that its basic preoccupation is Maggie Tulliver's struggle to come to terms both with herself and with the world in which she lives. In this struggle she is involved in three centrally important relationships—with her brother Tom, with Philip Wakem, and with Stephen Guest. And it is her unhappy destiny to find her struggle complicated and intensified rather than resolved by these ties. Only with death does she find release from her conflict, re-united with the brother who had so cruelly rejected her. It is in the light of her perennial struggle that everything in the novel must be viewed— her contacts with her relatives, her little private peculiarities, and her childish escapades. Mr and Mrs Glegg do not inhabit the book for their own sakes. They are there because they are part and parcel of the world in which Maggie sadly struggles.

95

We have now reached the point at which we may sketch an approach to one particular novel. Since we have been drawing examples from books already discussed to some extent in Chapter 4, we shall for this purpose choose another of them—Dickens's *Bleak House*.

We shall not attempt an exhaustive analysis of this book. It will be assumed that the reader, if he is not by this time acquainted with the book, will make it his business to become so. Our examination of parts of the novel will concentrate on setting up a few 'signposts', as it were, aimed at giving the reader his bearings, so that he may find his way to the significance of the unexamined portions by himself. The investigation of the book will therefore be based upon the highlighting of certain key passages, in which the author's dominant preoccupation is especially plain.

Like many other novels by Dickens, *Bleak House* has at its centre a specific social evil, the Court of Chancery, distinguished for its corruption, incompetence, and indolence. From its proceedings comes suffering rather than justice; suffering for those unlucky enough to be caught in its toils, vainly hoping for settlement. The Court of Chancery was concerned, most importantly, with matters in which the *law*, strictly interpreted, could give a definite ruling, but in which there might be some doubt as to whether or not the legal ruling satisfied the demands of *equity*, of reasonable humane fairness. Thus a man's will might decree that all his property should go to some person or institution quite unconnected with his family. Legally speaking, such a will would be held valid. But the widow of the deceased man, for instance, might seek to contest the will, in the interests of equity. She would then take the matter to the Court of Chancery. It is one of the ironies of *Bleak House* that a Court whose purpose was to help those to whom injustice had been done, is presented as a Court in which those who come to it for assistance are subjected to miseries as bad as or worse than those of a criminal in an ordinary court! The state of affairs Dickens deplored continued until 1873, when the Court of Chancery was reformed and reorganized. The first chapter of the novel, then, is appropriately entitled 'In Chancery'.

It begins with the description of a foggy day in London. This does more than simply create 'atmosphere'. Careful attention will reveal ingenious connections between features of the murky London scene and the Court of Chancery itself:

London. Michaelmas Term lately over, and the Lord Chancellor sitting in Lincoln's Inn Hall. Implacable November weather. As much mud in the streets, as if the waters had but newly retired from the face of the earth, and it would not be wonderful to meet a Megalosaurus, forty feet long or so, waddling like an elephantine lizard up Holborn Hill. Smoke lowering down from chimney-pots, making a soft, black drizzle, with flakes of soot in it as big as full-grown snowflakes—gone into mourning, one might imagine, for the death of the sun. Dogs, undistinguishable in mire. Horses, scarcely better; splashed to their very blinkers. Foot passengers, jostling one another's umbrellas, in a general infection of ill-temper, and losing their foothold at street corners, where tens of thousands of other foot passengers have been slipping and sliding since the day broke (if the day ever broke), adding new deposits to the crust upon crust of mud, sticking at those points tenaciously to the pavement, and accumulating at compound interest.

Fog everywhere. Fog up the river, where it flows among green aits and meadows; fog down the river, where it rolls defiled among the tiers of shipping, and the waterside pollutions of a great (and dirty) city....

When we look back at this opening from only a very few paragraphs later in the chapter, we are struck by a number of interesting points. If the November weather is 'Implacable', so, in the treatment of its victims, is the Court of Chancery itself. The Megalosaurus, too, has his place. This prehistoric monster is not brought in merely to provide an extravagantly decorative means of emphasizing the point about the mud in the streets. If he is prehistoric, so (metaphorically speaking) is an institution as outworn and superannuated as Chancery. And the mental picture of the creature 'waddling like an elephantine lizard up Holborn Hill' associates itself only too readily with the cumbersome, indeed 'elephantine' way, in which the Court goes about its business. The 'Foot passengers...losing their

4   97   M U L

foothold at street corners, where tens of thousands of other foot passengers have been slipping and sliding since the day broke', put us in mind of the many victims of Chancery who likewise lose their foothold—mentally and morally. As for the 'new deposits' added to the 'crust upon crust of mud', they link up with the deposits of legal 'mud', 'mountains of costly nonsense' as Dickens calls them, with which the Court is decked.

It is fitting that there should be 'Fog everywhere'. Fitting because, just as the fog rolls, creeps, and spreads, like some kind of hideous monster sending out inescapable tentacles, so the Court of Chancery spreads its malign influence into every corner of the country. As Dickens puts it a few paragraphs later, 'this is the Court of Chancery; which has its decaying houses and its blighted lands in every shire; which has its worn-out lunatic in every mad-house, and its dead in every churchyard; which has its ruined suitor, with his slipshod heels and threadbare dress, borrowing and begging through the round of every man's acquaintance....' No wonder that the Court should be found 'at the very heart of the fog':

The raw afternoon is rawest, and the dense fog is densest, and the muddy streets are muddiest, near the leaden-headed old obstruction, appropriate ornament for the threshold of a leaden-headed old corporation—Temple Bar. And hard by Temple Bar, in Lincoln's Inn Hall, at the very heart of the fog, sits the Lord High Chancellor in his High Court of Chancery.

But the fog does more than parallel the evil influence of the Court throughout the land. It also suggests the very manner in which Chancery's proceedings are conducted. For what have we here but a vast, thick, and seemingly endless legal 'fog'? The Lord High Chancellor is described as sitting 'with a *foggy* glory round his head...outwardly directing his contemplation to the lantern in the roof, where he can see nothing but *fog*', although he is supposed to be listening to the address of an advocate. The members of the High Court of Chancery bar present on this occasion are '*mistily* engaged in one of the ten thousand stages of an endless cause'. That is not all there is to be said about these gentlemen. They are, in addition, 'tripping one another up on slippery precedents' (a further parallel to the pedestrians 'losing their foothold at street corners'), and 'groping knee-deep in technicalities' (as the dogs of the first paragraph might be imagined to grope about in the mire). Before the various solicitors in the cause being heard lies a great agglomeration of legal junk: 'bills, cross-bills, answers, rejoinders, injunctions, affidavits, issues, references to masters, masters's reports, mountains of costly nonsense'. We shall be reminded of this legal rubbish-heap later in the book, in a superficially dissimilar but essentially remarkably similar context. 'Well may the court be dim,' says Dickens, 'with wasting candles here and there; well may the fog hang heavy in it, as if it would never get out....' If the candles are 'wasting', so are the lives of those whom the court is ruining. The fog this time has a double significance. On the one hand it can be taken as the legal fog which will 'never get out' because the Court of Chancery seems incapable of altering its ways. On the other hand the fog can be associated with the court's victims, who will 'never get out' because judgment will never, in their lifetime, be given on their suits.

This, then, is the Court of Chancery, 'which gives to monied might the means abundantly of wearying out the right; which so exhausts finances, patience, courage, hope; so overthrows the brain and breaks the heart; that there is not an honourable man among its practitioners who would not give—who does not often give—the warning, "Suffer any wrong that can be done you, rather than come here!"'

To approach *Bleak House* as though it were no more than an exposure of the iniquities of the Court of Chancery would, however, be a mistake. Everyone has been told at some time or other that Dickens was a social reformer. To deny that aspect of his work would certainly be foolish, but to overstress it is equally misguided. We do not need to read far in this novel to realize that the Court of Chancery, although it is at the centre of the book, is simply one example, if a monstrous one, of an evil that is more than 'social' in the usual sense. We have already spoken of the court's malign influence. It is by no means the sole representative of malignity in the book. Perhaps the best way to indicate its position, and at the same time to suggest how the novel is organized, is to compare the whole scheme with a *wheel*. The Court of Chancery is the hub of the wheel, while from this centre there radiates outwards a series of spokes. It is not hard to see a likeness between this way of looking at the court, and our earlier image of it as a monster with grasping tentacles. Once we have familiarized ourselves with this idea, we shall be able to see what Dickens is really concerned with in *Bleak House*.

This novel sets out to present, not a scheme of legal reform, but a particular vision of life. Although the book abounds in comedy, this vision is a sombre, even a savagely gloomy one. The vision is that of a world in which evil forces, with the Court of Chancery as their most vivid exemplar, fasten upon the good and the innocent, and grow fat by doing their utmost to squeeze the life-blood out of their victims. In fact it may be said that these are forces *actively contending against life itself.*

Let us return to our image of the wheel, as it will assist us in finding our way through this densely constructed book. If the Court of Chancery is the hub of the wheel, what of the spokes? Now, some of these 'spokes' have a very obvious connection with Chancery, and it would therefore be logical to consider them first. One of them, though it might superficially appear remote from the court and its doings, is the subject of the second chapter, 'In fashion'. Dickens is careful to establish the connection, both by the parallel between the titles of this chapter and its predecessor, and by what he actually has to tell us in the opening paragraph:

It is but a glimpse of the world of fashion that we want on this same miry afternoon. It is not so unlike the Court of Chancery, but that we may pass from the one scene to the other, as the crow flies. Both the world of fashion and the Court of Chancery are things of precedent and usage: oversleeping Rip Van Winkles, who have played at strange games through a deal of thundery weather; sleeping beauties, whom the Knight will wake one day, when all the stopped spits in the kitchen shall begin to turn prodigiously!

To this world belong Sir Leicester and Lady Dedlock, who will be so mysteriously and, in the end, tragically involved in the story of the heroine of the novel, Esther Summerson. One feature of the way in which Dickens goes on to speak about this world needs special mention, as it is connected with an idea recurring, sometimes quite explicitly, at other times by implication, throughout the book:

There is much good in it; there are many good and true people in it; it has its appointed place. But the evil of it is, that it is a world wrapped up in too much jeweller's cotton and fine wool, and cannot hear the rushing of the larger worlds, and cannot see them as they circle round the sun. It is a deadened world, and its growth is sometimes unhealthy for want of air.

In our previous chapter we encountered the Smallweed family, and we observed that just as weeds strangle the growth of healthy plants, so these people exist by fastening upon unwary and unfortunate humans, and squeezing them dry. The 'stump of an old forest tree', found so surprisingly lingering in the street they inhabit, is a parallel to the lives the Smallweeds have blighted. The words Dickens uses in describing the world of fashion have somewhat similar associations: 'It is a *deadened* world, and its *growth* is sometimes *unhealthy* for want of air'. We shall see this 'deadness' and 'unhealthiness' clinging to other 'spokes' in the wheel.

Who, for instance, could seem more thoroughly unhealthy and essentially 'dead' than Mr Krook, landlord of Miss Flite, the 'little mad old woman in a squeezed bonnet, who is always in court, from its sitting to its rising, and always expecting some incomprehensible judgment to be given in her favour'? This is how Esther Summerson sees him:

Turning towards the door, he now caught sight of us. He was short, cadaverous, and withered; with his head sunk in visible smoke from his mouth, as if he were on fire within. His throat, chin and eyebrows were so frosted with white hairs, and so gnarled with veins and puckered skin, that he looked from his breast upward like some old root in a fall of snow.

His fate will abundantly bear out our first impressions of him. But the shop he keeps is as odd and interesting as the man himself:

She had stopped at a shop, over which was written, KROOK, RAG AND BOTTLE WAREHOUSE. Also, in long thin letters, KROOK, DEALER IN MARINE STORES. In one part of the window was a picture of a red paper mill, at which a cart was unloading a quantity of sacks of old rags. In another, was the inscription, BONES BOUGHT. In another, KITCHEN-STUFF BOUGHT. In another, OLD IRON BOUGHT. In another, WASTE PAPER BOUGHT. In another, LADIES' AND GENTLEMEN'S WARDROBES BOUGHT. Everything seemed to be bought, and nothing to be sold there. In all parts of the window, were quantities of dirty bottles—blacking bottles, medicine bottles, ginger-beer and soda-water bottles, pickle bottles, wine bottles, ink bottles: I am reminded by mentioning the latter, that the shop had, in several little particulars, the air of being in a legal neighbourhood, and of being, as it were, a dirty hanger-on and disowned relation of the law. There were a great many ink bottles. There was a little tottering bench of shabby old volumes outside the door, labelled 'Law Books, all at 9*d*.'... There were several second-hand bags, blue and red, hanging up. A little way within the shop-door, lay heaps of old crackled parchment scrolls, and discoloured and dog's-eared law-papers. I could have fancied that all the rusty keys, of which there must have been hundreds huddled together as old iron, had once belonged to doors of rooms or strong chests in lawyers' offices. The litter of rags tumbled partly into and partly out of a one-legged wooden scale, hanging without any counterpoise from a beam, might have been counsellors' bands and gowns torn up. One had only to fancy, as Richard whispered to Ada and me while we all stood looking in, that yonder bones in a corner, piled together and picked very clean, were the bones of clients, to make the picture complete.

It does not take much stretching of the imagination to associate this collection of rubbish with the 'mountains of costly nonsense' piled before the solicitors in the Court of Chancery. We are hardly surprised, then, when Mr Krook says 'they call me the Lord Chancellor, and call my shop Chancery'.

'You see I have so many things here,' he resumed, holding up the lantern, 'of so many kinds, and all as the neighbours think (but *they* know nothing), wasting away and going to rack and ruin, and that's why they have given me and my place a christening. And I have so many old parchmentses and papers in my stock. And I have a liking for rust and must and

102

cobwebs. And all's fish that comes to my net. And I can't bear to part with anything I once lay hold of (or so my neighbours think, but what do *they* know?) or to alter anything or to have any sweeping, nor scouring, nor cleaning, nor repairing going on about me. That's the way I've got the ill name of Chancery. I don't mind. I go to see my noble and learned brother well every day, when he sits in the Inn. He don't notice me, but I notice him. There's no great odds betwixt us. We both grub on in a muddle....'

Thus Mr Krook's death in Chapter 32, the result of his prodigious drinking habits, though it taxes our ability to believe that such a thing could happen in 'real life', is imaginatively absolutely right. Tony Weevle and Mr Guppy, in search of Krook, find in his room nothing but his horribly charred remains:

The Lord Chancellor of that Court, true to his title in his last act, has died the death of all Lord Chancellors in all Courts, and of all authorities in all places under all names soever, where false pretences are made, and where injustice is done. Call the death by any name Your Highness will, attribute it to whom you will, or say it might have been prevented how you will, it is the same death eternally—inborn, inbred, engendered in the corrupted humours of the vicious body itself, and that only—Spontaneous Combustion, and none other of all the deaths that can be died.

The Court of Chancery, all that it represents, and everything associated with it, must therefore, sooner or later, die as Mr Krook has died, from inner rottenness.

We could, if we wished, go on to consider other 'spokes' of the wheel obviously related to the Court of Chancery. It will, however, be left to the reader himself to identify them and see how they fit into the overall scheme. Our attention must now be devoted to the 'spokes' whose relation to the court is by no means plain at first sight. Among these is Mr Harold Skimpole, 'a little bright creature, with a rather large head; but a delicate face, and a sweet voice, and there was a perfect charm in him. All he said was so free from effort and spontaneous, and was said with such a captivating gaiety, that it was fascinating to hear him talk.' Yet Skimpole, superficially so delightful, is one of the sinister characters of the novel. He, like the Smallweeds, is a parasite; a parasite upon the innocent generosity of Mr Jarndyce, a parasite who achieves his success by captivating those who meet him, with an apparently ingenuous candour:

'I covet nothing....Possession is nothing to me. Here is my friend Jarndyce's excellent house. I feel obliged to him for possessing it. I can sketch it, and alter it, and alter it. I can set it to music. When I am here, I have sufficient possession of it, and have neither trouble, cost, nor responsibility....'

Why do we associate him with the Court of Chancery? Precisely because he, like the court, exemplifies those evil forces in humanity which seek their own good by the exploitation of others. And he strikes us as all the more evil for his carefully cultivated air of childlike innocence.

Another 'spoke' in the wheel is old Mr Turveydrop, the father of the young man to whom Caddy Jellyby is engaged to be married. His very appearance, with its elaborate artificiality, is as full of 'false pretences' as the Court of Chancery itself:

He was a fat old gentleman with a false complexion, false teeth, false whiskers, and a wig. He had a fur collar, and he had a padded breast to his coat, which only wanted a star or a broad blue ribbon to be complete. He was pinched in, and swelled out, and got up, and strapped down, as much as he could possibly bear. He had a neckcloth on (puffing his very eyes out of their natural shape), and his chin and even his ears so sunk into it, that it seemed as though he must inevitably double up, if it were cast loose. He had, under his arm, a hat of great size and weight, shelving downward from the crown to the brim; and in his hand a pair of white gloves, with which he flapped it, as he stood poised on one leg, in a high shouldered, round elbowed state of elegance not to be surpassed. He had a cane, he had an eye-glass, he had a snuff-box, he had rings, he had wristbands, he had everything but any touch of nature; he was not like youth, he was not like age, he was not like anything in the world but a model of Deportment.

To exhibit himself in the most fashionable places, and to maintain his would-be aristocratic and ludicrously exaggerated elegance, is Mr Turveydrop's only consideration in life. Other people are important to him only in so far as they flatter him for his spurious gentility, or contribute, like his unfortunate family, to the upkeep of its conspicuous signs:

He had married a meek little dancing-mistress, with a tolerable connection (having never in his life done anything but deport himself), and had worked her to death, or had, at the best, suffered her to work herself to death, to maintain him in those expenses which were indispensable to his position. At once to exhibit his Deportment to the best models, and to keep the best models constantly before himself, he had found it necessary to frequent all public places of fashionable and lounging resort; to be seen at Brighton and elsewhere at fashionable times; and to lead an idle life in the very best clothes. To enable him to do this, the affectionate little dancing-mistress had toiled and laboured, and would have toiled and laboured to that hour, if her strength had lasted so long. For, the mainspring of the story was, that, in spite of the man's absorbing selfishness, his wife (overpowered by his Deportment) had, to the last, believed in him, and had, on her death-bed, in the most moving terms, confided him to their son as one who had an inextinguishable claim upon him, and whom he could never regard with too much pride and deference. The son, inheriting his mother's belief, and having the Deportment always before him, had lived and grown in the same faith, and now, at thirty years of age, worked for his father twelve hours a-day, and looked up to him with veneration on the old imaginary pinnacle.

Thus Mr Turveydrop is another parasite, another person who, in his utterly blatant self-seeking, is growing fat upon the lives of others. And, in being this kind of man, he reveals himself as one more ally of the Court of Chancery.

There are a good many of the court's allies to be found in rather unexpected corners. Take, for example, that canting hypocrite Mr Chadband, who justifies his own piggish gluttony in a preposterous caricature of a sermon:

'I say, my friends,' pursues Mr. Chadband,...'why can we not fly? Is it because we are calculated to walk? It is. Could we walk, my friends, without strength? We could not. What should we do without strength, my friends? Our legs would refuse to bear us, our knees would double up, our ankles would turn over, and we should come to the ground. Thence from whence, my friends, in a human point of view, de we derive the strength that is necessary to our limbs? Is it,' says Chadband, glancing over the table, 'from bread in various forms, from butter which is churned from the milk which is yielded unto us by the cow, from the eggs which are laid by the fowl, from ham, from tongue, from sausage, and from such like? It is. Then let us partake of the good things which are before us!'

Mr Chadband resembles the Court of Chancery in being a sham. His brand of oratory is as hollow and futile as the legal mouthings of the lawyers in the court. The fact that he is comic does not make him any the less repulsive.

Comic also, but likewise a 'spoke', firmly attached to the hub of the wheel, is Mrs Jellyby, engrossed in a fantastic project for developing the region of Borrioboola-Gha, 'on the left bank of the Niger'. The fact that she has never been there, and is never likely to go there at all, is very far from occurring to this lady as anything in the way of a disadvantage. Surrounded by a voluminous and perpetually increasing correspondence, eternally visited by cranks full of idiotic new schemes for the Borrioboola-Gha project, she lets her home go to slatternly ruin, and cheerfully ignores the well-being of her family. Her daughter Caddy, painfully aware of the disgraceful condition of the house, is forever being called upon to write letters (connected, of course, with the project) for her mother. Mrs Jellyby is supposed to be a woman with a 'mission', an organizer of philanthropy. Esther Summerson hears her engage in a discussion with a certain Mr Quale on the Brotherhood of Humanity, and give utterance 'to some beautiful sentiments'. But these 'sentiments' are in reality no less hollow than the oratory of Mr Chadband. What can Mrs Jellyby actually feel about the Brotherhood of Humanity if she is contented with the state of her own hard-driven daughter?

But what principally struck us was a jaded, and unhealthy-looking, though by no means plain girl, at the writing-table, who sat biting the feather of her pen, and staring at us. I suppose nobody ever was in such a state of ink. And, from her tumbled hair to her pretty feet, which were disfigured with frayed and broken satin slippers trodden down at heel, she really seemed to have no article of dress upon her, from a pin upwards, that was in its proper condition or its right place.

Well may she look *unhealthy*. The effulgently benevolent Mrs Jellyby, the fount of 'beautiful sentiments', has no time for benevolence at home. Caddy is in fact as miserably exploited as the young man to whom she becomes engaged is exploited by Mr Turveydrop.

Mrs Jellyby is not the only person of this particular type in *Bleak House*. Just as Mr Jarndyce is cold-bloodedly made use of by Harold Skimpole, so is he exposed to the onslaught of a horde of ladies distinguished, as Dickens puts it, for 'rapacious benevolence'. Demands are always being made upon his generosity by these incredibly energetic females, who seem to have nothing else to do in life except organize one philanthropic project after another. Dickens is not laughing at genuine philanthropy; but he describes the activities of these people in such a way as to convince us that their benevolence is no more real than the justice of the Court of Chancery:

They threw themselves into committees in the most impassioned manner, and collected subscriptions with a vehemence quite extraordinary. It appeared to us that some of them must pass their whole lives in dealing out subscription-cards to the whole Post-Office Directory—shilling cards, half-crown cards, half-sovereign cards, penny cards. They wanted everything. They wanted wearing apparel, they wanted linen rags, they wanted money, they wanted coals, they wanted soup, they wanted interest, they wanted autographs, they wanted flannel, they wanted whatever Mr. Jarndyce had—or had not. Their objects were as various as their demands. They were going to raise new buildings, they were going to pay off debts on old buildings, they were going to establish in a picturesque building (engraving of proposed West Elevation attached) the Sisterhood of Mediaeval Marys; they were going to give a testimonial to Mrs. Jellyby; they were going to have their Secretary's portrait painted, and presented to his mother-in-law, whose deep devotion to him was well known; they were going to get up everything, I really believe, from five hundred thousand tracts to an annuity, and from a marble monument to a silver tea-pot.

Somehow the words 'mountains of costly nonsense' recur to us as we go through this catalogue of objects and demands.

By this time the status of the Smallweed family in the scheme of the novel will have grown apparent to the reader. They can almost be looked upon as a kind of Court of Chancery in miniature, so intent are they upon the pursuit of their victims, and so utterly relentless in their treatment of them. The image of great-grandfather Smallweed as 'a horny-skinned, two-legged, money-getting species of spider, who spun webs to catch unwary flies' now seems especially apt. The 'unwary flies' are first cousins to the people whose lives the court has ruined.

A great deal more could, of course, be said about *Bleak House*. Further characters could be isolated for scrutiny, and whole episodes could be examined for the way in which the central vision of the novel is projected. Enough should have been done, however, to indicate the main lines along which a profitable study of the book ought to proceed. To seize upon the guiding principle of a novel, to diagnose the nature of the central preoccupation so that one may see every part of the work in relation to it—that is the essential. To do this requires flexibility in the reader, as he cannot expect every novel to yield the same kind of analysis. Sometimes (though not often) the central preoccupation will be the fairly simple presentation of a moral dictum—as in Samuel Johnson's *Rasselas*, which has a similar theme to his poem *The Vanity of Human Wishes*. Or it may be, as in the case of *Bleak House* and *The Mayor of Casterbridge*, that the author has what we might call a particular slant upon life, which he wishes to embody in a work of art. It may even be a matter of *a special way of telling a story*—but to discuss novels of that type, exciting though they are, would be to take us beyond the limits of this introductory study.

PART III

6. THE ELEMENTS OF POETRY

In Chapter 2 we looked closely at certain aspects of a poem by Wordsworth called *The Solitary Reaper*, and in the chapter following we
made an examination of a ballad. Yet it may already have occurred to
the reader that something was missing on both the occasions when
we gave our attention to poetry. He may well object that there was
really nothing said about *The Solitary Reaper* or *The Demon Lover*
that might not have been said about a work written in prose. True,
reference was made to 'lines', and 'stanzas'; but, apart from this,
how much was there in the account of either poem that had to do
with its specifically *poetic* qualities? Was any point made about the
handling of verse? Was there, in fact, any indication that *The Solitary
Reaper* or *The Demon Lover* had to be written in verse to achieve the
effects we found in them? Indeed, the reader might feel tempted
to ask why verse should be used at all, if prose will do equally
well.

Perhaps he will after all admit that there is one obvious reason
why the story of *The Demon Lover* had to be cast in verse. What we
have in that ballad is the words of a song, and the words of a song
are usually thought of as being written in verse. However, there are
two stanzas in this poem to which it is worth returning, as they
suggest something more than a pleasant jingle to gratify the singing
voice:

> She had not sailed a league, a league,
>   A league but barely three,
> When dismal grew his countenance,
>   And drumlie grew his ee.

> They had not sailed a league, a league,
>   A league but barely three,
> Until she espied his cloven foot,
>   And she wept right bitterlie.

We are here approaching the climax of the poem. So far there have been indications of something uncanny about the ship. Now the true nature of her owner is revealed. It is therefore to be expected that the poem will at this point make some show of building up suspense. And this is precisely what is done, by extremely simple means, in the first two lines of each stanza. If you read these stanzas aloud— and, as we shall see, all poetry is meant to be read aloud—you will notice that the first two lines have in each case a heavy, insistent *beat*:

> She had not sailed a *lea*gue, a *lea*gue,
> A *lea*gue but barely *three*.

There is a feeling of relentlessness generated by this, a sense that the woman is being irrevocably driven to a sinister destiny. Consider also the effect produced by the almost exact repetition of the lines in the second of these stanzas. The first stanza of the pair has ended on a decidedly threatening note. We are wondering what will happen next. And the suspense is increased in a masterly way by the interruption of the story for two lines, in which the insistent pulse of the verse seems more ominous than ever. We almost feel like saying, 'For goodness sake stop repeating yourself, and go on and tell us what *happened*'; but the interruption makes the revelation of the demon's cloven foot, when it comes, doubly frightening.

If the use of verse can be as telling as that in a simple ballad— though, as our analysis of it showed, the simplicity may be deceptive—it can do a great deal more in the very finest poetry. We do not propose in this chapter to make a schematic survey of the different ingredients of poetry, drawing examples from a variety of poets. Some idea of the variety of poetry will be given in the concluding chapter. What we shall do now is examine one short poem in minute detail, discussing the various poetic ingredients revealed by it, as they come before our attention. The poem we have chosen is one of the 'Holy Sonnets' by the seventeenth-century poet John Donne:

> Thou hast made me, and shall thy work decay?
> Repair me now, for now mine end doth haste,

I run to death, and death meets me as fast,
And all my pleasures are like yesterday;
I dare not move my dim eyes any way,
Despair behind, and death before doth cast
Such terror, and my feeble flesh doth waste
By sin in it, which it t'wards hell doth weigh;
Only thou art above, and when towards thee
By thy leave I can look, I rise again;
But our old subtle foe so tempteth me,
That not one hour my self I can sustain;
Thy Grace may wing me to prevent his art,
And thou like Adamant draw mine iron heart.

This is a very different kind of poem from *The Demon Lover*. To start with the most obvious point, it is not anonymous. Instead of being the work of generations of folk-singers modifying some far-off original song, it is the production of one individual literary artist.

That in itself makes for all manner of differences, but we shall concern ourselves now with the two main ones alone. The first difference is that whereas in *The Demon Lover* we do not feel that the original poet, whoever he may have been, wrote the poem because of some deeply felt personal experience he had undergone, in Donne's poem we do feel this. *The Demon Lover* gives us a story with an implied 'moral'. It is, of course, just possible that the person whom we may imagine to have written the original version *might* have known temptation similar to the kind offered to the woman in the poem, but the speculation is an idle one, as there is not the slightest hint of such a possibility in the ballad itself. We have no sense of the poet saying 'Look, this is what has happened to *me*!' To put it another way, we do not feel that he is personally involved in the story. In 'Thou hast made me', on the other hand, John Donne seems not only to be making poetry out of urgent and poignant personal experience, but to be actually going through the experience as we read the poem. He seems to be saying not so much 'Look, this is what has happened to me, and what fine poetry I have made out of it!' as 'Look at what *is happening to me*!'

This does not mean that Donne was in fact going through that precise experience while writing the poem. Indeed that is exceedingly unlikely, as such experiences are too engrossing to leave any room for literary artistry when a man is actually living through them. Yet, however great or small the time separating the experience itself from the writing of the poem, Donne's poetic art has such power that the impression we receive is that the experience is being lived through at this very moment. In other words, the poem gives an effect of tremendous *immediacy*.

As soon as we begin to talk about 'Donne's poetic art', we find ourselves face to face with the second of the two great differences between 'Thou hast made me' and *The Demon Lover*: Donne's poem is a work of literary art in a sense in which *The Demon Lover* is not.

Now what do we mean by saying this? To begin with, 'Thou hast made me' is a sonnet. The sonnet is a kind of poem, a *literary form*, introduced into England from Italy during the sixteenth century. The most famous sonnets, like those of Shakespeare and the present poem by Donne, consist of fourteen lines, of which the first eight are called the *octave*, and the last six the *sestet*. Though there can be departures from this scheme, it remains the basic and most usual pattern. In a ballad there can be any number of lines, so it follows that the sonnet, by contrast with the ballad, is a form which imposes restrictions on the writer. Because of this, the sonnet is a literary form which offers a challenge to the poet who uses it. It gives him only a narrow space in which to work, and challenges him to exercise to the utmost his poetic skill, so as to pack as much meaning as possible into those mere fourteen lines. Thus part of the admiration aroused by a good sonnet, though only part of it, will be admiration for the poet's skill in doing so much within so small a space.

But we are not yet at the root of the difference between our two poems. After all, we cannot properly speak of the ballad as a form which does not impose any restrictions on the writer. For one thing the very fact that a ballad is meant to be sung imposes a kind of restriction, as the language must be extremely direct and simple if the meaning of the words is to be taken in as well as the music. And, furthermore, a ballad is far from being the only kind of poem which differs from a sonnet in that it can have any number of lines. And it would not be correct to say that the sonnet is the only kind of poem in which the writer is conscious of restrictions.

The truth is that the type of poem we call a sonnet is an extreme example of the general difference between folk-song and poetry written by individual literary artists like Shakespeare, Milton, Keats, or Donne. I have said that admiration for the skill displayed by the poet will account for part of the enthusiasm a reader will feel for a good sonnet. Obviously the kind of skill involved here, the skill which enables the poet to pack so much into so small a space, is skill in the expressive use of language. Now, admiration for a man's skill in using language is not something felt only by readers of sonnets. It is not even felt only by readers. Consider the admiration which can be awakened by a great public speaker, for instance, or, returning to the ballad, by the skill of a resourceful folk-singer giving some striking new twist to a ballad already familiar to those who are listening to him. And admiration of this kind may be aroused by things other than language—by music, by an exquisite piece of carving, or the weaving of a fine cloth.

Now it is plain that a carver or a weaver, to take only two of the many possible examples, must be in a particularly good position to appreciate a fine piece of work done by a fellow-practitioner of his craft; but that does not make him the only kind of person who has a right to say what he thinks about it. People who are themselves quite unable to carve or weave, yet have been accustomed to seeing the products of carving or weaving all their lives, will know what is good and what is not good simply because their familiarity with these things has given them standards by which to judge. Carving or weaving are part of the surroundings those people have always known, so they really do understand what they are talking about. In the same way, you do not need to be a poet in order to recognize and enjoy a good sonnet when you see one, or indeed any other sort of poem; but you do need to have some idea of what you are talking about.

Knowing what you are talking about, when it comes to poetry, can be the result of one of two things. Either you have always lived among people who regard poetry as one of life's enjoyments, so that you have more or less unconsciously acquired their ideas and standards; or, if your life has been passed mainly among those who are ignorant of poetry, or even hostile towards it, you may find your interest awakened by a book, a teacher, an article, a person outside the immediate group in which you live, and this may make you go on consciously to seek guidance that will help you to arrive at ideas and standards.

The point I want to make is that, just as there are people who know and appreciate a fine piece of weaving when they see it, because weaving is part of their surroundings, part of the very 'atmosphere' they live in, so there are people who know and appreciate a good poem when they see it, because poetry is part of the 'atmosphere' of their lives. This will rarely be because they actually live among people writing poetry, but will depend on one of the two causes we have outlined. It is to people like this that such a poem as 'Thou hast made me' makes its appeal, people who understand and enjoy masterly handling of language when they come across it, and who admire a poet's successful use of a challenging form not simply because of the 'technical' skill he shows, but because in his use of that form he has managed to give the reader a thrilling experience. For the man who enjoys poetry, a fine poem is not merely something he reads and forgets about; it is a vivid experience, an event in his life.

To help the reader of this book to know what he is talking about when it comes to poetry is the object of this section. Before we actually come to grips with 'Thou hast made me', there is a further point to be made. As soon as we start using the words 'masterly handling of language', and 'successful use of a challenging form', we find ourselves indicating the fundamental reason for saying that 'Thou hast made me' is a work of literary art in a sense in which *The Demon Lover* is not. It should not be supposed that the language of *The Demon Lover* is in any way feeble or incompetent. On the contrary, it is admirably suited to its purpose. Indeed, the way in which the story's implied moral significance is conveyed shows a high artistry of a certain kind. You will remember what we found to say about those simple words 'No mariners could she behold'. But what we did *not* find ourselves doing was making any comment on such things as 'tone', or 'movement'. The poem did not call for it. The tone of voice we may imagine to be adopted by the characters at different stages of the dialogue is such an obvious matter ('saucy', 'bitter', 'fearful', 'threatening', according to the context) that it does not need special comment. As for 'movement', the topic will arise as soon as we begin our examination of 'Thou hast made me'.

To sum up, then: the two great points of difference between the poems are that (*a*) Donne's poem is the work of a single individual, and conveys an impression of strong personal feeling, whereas *The Demon Lover*, in being handed down from generation to generation, is really the work of a number of different people living at different times, and does not express personal feeling, but is, as we say, 'impersonal'; and that (*b*) 'Thou hast made me', in conveying intense personal feeling, makes far more use of the resources and peculiarities of language, and the possibilities of verse, than *The Demon Lover*. As we have seen, there is plenty to interest us in a good ballad, but it does not exploit the potentialities of words as Donne's poem does. Donne is acutely aware of what words can do, and he uses them as deliberately as a painter uses lines and colours.

Let us now pass to the poem itself. The opening line falls into halves, the first of which is a statement: 'Thou hast made me'. Directly addressing his God, the poet is asserting something which he, as a Christian, believes. Whatever else may be confused and uncertain, *that*, at any rate, gives him a feeling of complete assurance. Try actually speaking the words aloud. You will find that you cannot comfortably say them quickly. It is quite easy to see why this is so. There is no difficulty about saying the words 'Thou hast' quickly, one after the other; but it is not possible to say 'hast made me' in the same way. Or rather, it is not possible to do so without making the words sound clumsy and awkward. The explanation lies in the movements we have to make with the tongue and lips in order clearly to articulate the words. Passing from the 't' at the end of 'hast' to the 'm' at the beginning of 'made' forces the speaker to make radical changes in oral positioning. The tongue has to be brought cleanly away from the teeth before the lips come together, and if we try to do this too fast we shall not be able to articulate the words distinctly. There is a similar change when we move from the end of 'made' to the beginning of 'me'. Instead of saying all the words quickly together, then, we have to move deliberately, and detach them from one another.

The effect is reminiscent of the children's party game of 'tongue-twisters'. Each person taking part is made to say something awkward, like 'Run rat, leap rat', three times quickly in succession. The chances are that he will find himself hopelessly entangled, just because of the changes of position he has to make with his mouth. Probably no one would have quite that difficulty with the words 'Thou hast made me', however quickly he said them; but they would sound blurred and unsatisfactory all the same. It is, in fact, impossible to overestimate the importance to poetry of the effects produced by the speed or slowness with which words can be distinctly articulated. It is the chief controlling factor in what we call *movement*. Words may be spoken one after the other in rapid succession, or else slowly and deliberately detached from each other according to the ease or difficulty involved in passing from one word to the next. And, of course, there are all the various degrees of speed or slowness, depending upon the various degrees of ease or difficulty in the articulation.

Perhaps few poets have ever consciously worked out their effects of movement by saying to themselves, 'It is hard to say a word beginning with "m" quickly after a word ending in "t"', or whatever the case may be. But a poet instinctively knows that certain words will move quickly and easily together, whilst others will not. And his ability to control the movement of his verse is one of the most valuable and powerful means of expression in his equipment.

Take the present instance. We have observed that in these four words, 'Thou hast made me', Donne is asserting something which he, as a Christian, believes to be true. He experiences, and wishes to communicate, a feeling of complete assurance in this, if in nothing else. And how powerfully this comes out in the movement! Moving with slow deliberation, the words give an effect of tremendous *weight*, so that we are made to feel the whole force of Donne's assurance.

Though each word is heavily emphasized, it is the word 'made' that receives the greatest stress, as you will have noticed in speaking the sentence aloud. It is God as 'maker' that Donne is addressing. In the second half of the line he is still addressing God the maker, but with a difference. For the second half takes the form of a question: 'and shall thy work decay?' Now, the very fact that it is a question makes a difference. A question, after all, means that the person who asks it is uncertain about something. So, if the statement in the first half of the line conveys assurance, the question in the second half brings in a hint of uncertainty.

There is, however, a certain type of question which is not really a question at all, but a way of making a statement. We may, if we wish, take Donne's question as an example, in which case 'and shall thy work decay?' can be regarded as a dramatic way of saying 'Thy work shall *not* decay!' We could as easily rewrite the opening statement as a question—'Hast thou not made me?'

But the fact remains that a question is a question, and because a question may have more than one answer, it must inevitably suggest the possibility of things being uncertain. Donne certainly intends his question to be in *part* a disguised statement. He is trying to keep up the mood of assurance expressed in the first half of the line. When we move on to the rest of the poem, however, we realize that we also have to take it as a real question, to which the answer may well turn out to be 'Yes!' God's work as the maker of John

Donne will decay unless John Donne, with the help of God, is able to overcome sin and the temptation to despair. Thus the question in the first line in one way carries on the assurance of the very opening, and in another way prepares us for the torment which follows in the rest of the poem.

In the second line, Donne calls upon God to 'repair' him, to make him fit to confront death and judgment. It is useful to take the second, third, and fourth lines together:

> Repair me now, for now mine end doth haste,
> I run to death, and death meets me as fast,
> And all my pleasures are like yesterday;

Which words stand out most obviously in these lines? Plainly they are 'now' and 'death', simply because they are repeated. Donne is not making these repetitions for lack of something to say. The repetition of 'now' gives an impression of great urgency. It is as though Donne were saying 'If anything can be done to save me, it must be done NOW!' In the same way, the repetition of 'death' brings home to us just how terrifyingly close death seems to the poet.

Observe how the *movement*, in the first half of the second of these lines, suggests a headlong rush towards death—'I run to death'. There is no difficulty here in moving from word to word. What is the meaning of the last of this group of lines? How are we intended to take the word 'pleasures'? From the rest of the poem it is clear that Donne means 'worldly' pleasures, pleasures of the flesh, no doubt, which he has enjoyed in the past, and which now come flooding back into his mind with terrible vividness, as though he had experienced them only 'yesterday'. All the sins of his past life seem present to him as death quickly and relentlessly draws near.

Let us take the next four lines together as a group:

> I dare not move my dim eyes any way,
> Despair behind, and death before doth cast
> Such terror, and my feeble flesh doth waste
> By sin in it, which it t'wards hell doth weigh;

In the first two of these lines we have a splendid example of what can be done through the handling of movement. Donne is saying that whichever way he might look, whether 'behind' or 'before', he would be sure to see something terrifying—despair on the one hand, death on the other. Of course, he would not actually *see* either death or despair. What he means is that if he thinks back to his past life, the recollection of his sins drives him to despair; and if he thinks forward to the future he can be aware of one thing only—impending death. But death and despair are so dreadfully real to him that they seem like physical shapes which he would see if he dared to gaze around. Now, much of the force of the lines comes from the slow, clogged movement. Instead of moving with the speed and impetuosity of 'I run to death', the first line of this group is for the most part slow and heavy. It is easy enough to say 'I dare not' and 'any way' quickly, but to say 'not move my dim eyes' properly requires quite an effort. Even 'any way' has to be said quite slowly if we are to bring out the meaning correctly. For the words do not mean the same thing as 'anyway'. They mean here, 'either this way or that way'. So they must be carefully detached from one another: '*any* way'.

Thus the very meaning of words, as well as the ease or difficulty involved in articulating them, may affect movement. Look at the words 'dim eyes'. Nothing could be easier than slurring one word into the next: 'dimeyes'. But how silly and slovenly it sounds! How confusing, too, for the two words might well be taken in such a reading for the one word 'demise', which here makes nonsense. Once more the words must be detached from one another if they are to be intelligible.

All this makes the movement slow and heavy. It seems weighed down with a burden, almost fixed to the spot. The significance of this becomes plain at the end of the four lines, when we actually reach the word 'weigh'. It is a burden of sin, which Donne feels to be dragging him down to hell. As for the sense of being fixed to the spot, it is so effective because Donne's eyes *are* fixed, for he dare not move them either this way or that. So the very movement of the verse suggests what the words are saying. Or, to put this idea in a more handy form, we can say that the movement *enacts* the meaning.

We must now look carefully at the second line of our group of four; or rather, the second line and the beginning of the third. For here we have something new. Up to now we have met only 'end-stopped' lines; that is to say, lines ending either with a definite and necessary pause in the flow of what is being said, a punctuation mark, or consisting of a complete sentence. 'Repair me now, for now mine end doth haste', for example, is complete in itself, so that it is possible to make quite a long pause at the end of the line without breaking the flow of the sense. But in the case we are now examining the sense spills over from one line into the next. It is not complete till we reach the words 'Such terror'. In fact, what we have here is a 'run-on' line.

We shall discuss the subject of run-on lines at some length, as it is of the utmost importance. The great test of a speaker of poetry is his ability to deal with run-on lines correctly. Very few—and this unfortunately includes many professional Shakespearian actors— adequately pass this test, yet there is no real difficulty and certainly no mystery about the business. Let us consider two alternative ways of dealing with our particular example:

> Despair behind, and death before doth cast
> Such terror,

Suppose we treated it as we would an end-stopped line. That would mean making a decided pause after 'cast', and dropping the voice on that word; after which the words 'Such terror' would follow as though they were the beginning of a fresh sentence, and had nothing to do with what had gone before: 'Despair behind, and death before doth cast. Such terror...'. Obviously it is absurd.

Now let us try going to the opposite extreme. Suppose we speak the words without making the slightest pause after 'cast': 'Despair behind, and death before doth cast such terror'. That is certainly preferable to the other reading, as it does preserve the shape of the sentence. But it is open to one very serious criticism. If we speak the words in that way, we are speaking them as though they were part of a piece of prose, whereas Donne happens to have written a poem. As it is reasonable to assume that Donne knew what he was doing when he chose to write this poem, we may assume further that he was aiming at some particular effect in making the sense run over from one line into the next—an effect possible only in poetry, and not in prose.

The words of a poem are arranged as they are for a good reason, not because the poet thought they would make a pretty design on paper. A very great deal of poetry, though by no means all of it, makes use of *metre*. In such poetry, each line will follow a pattern of unstressed and stressed syllables. It will divide into a certain number of 'feet'. All the lines in 'Thou hast made me' are founded on the same pattern of syllables. Probably you will already have recognized this pattern as what is called the iambic pentameter:

$$\breve{\text{Repair}} \mid \text{mĕ nōw}, \mid \text{fŏr nōw} \mid \text{mĭne ēnd} \mid \text{dŏth hāste},$$

In *The Demon Lover*, on the other hand, we find a line made up of four feet alternating with a line consisting of three, throughout the poem:

$$\text{'Ŏ whēre} \mid \text{hăve yŏu bēen,} \mid \text{mў lōng,} \mid \text{lŏng lōve,}$$
$$\text{Thĭs lōng} \mid \text{sĕvĕn yēars} \mid \text{ănd māir?'}$$

But whether the lines of a poem are varied or uniform in length is unimportant. What matters is that each line, as far as the metre is concerned, is a complete whole. The line 'Repair me now, for now mine end doth haste', makes up a complete series of five feet. In the next line, 'I run to death, and death meets me as fast', the poet starts again and gives us another complete series of five feet. And so on all the way through the poem. If we are looking simply at the metre, and ignoring the meaning, we can see each line standing by itself as a complete series of five feet.

This, then, is the way in which Donne has chosen to arrange the words of his poem, and we return to the assumption that he did so for a good reason. Like most good reasons, it is a simple one. He has arranged his words in a sequence of lines, each consisting of five feet, because the metre is one of the means by which he is able *to control and direct the way in which the words are to be read.* As we shall see, the actual sense of the words, what they mean, the way in which we feel they should 'go', are also determining factors affecting our reading of them. We observe further that a poet again and again achieves powerful effects by playing off the sense of the words against the metre. He will indeed use metre so that his words will be read exactly as he wishes them to be read—provided, of course, that the reader is attentive to the way in which he has arranged them. He may want a light stress in one place, a heavy emphasis in another; a decided break here, a small hesitation there. Prose can hardly do this for him; certainly not with anything like the same exactitude.

We did not find it necessary to mention metre when we examined *The Demon Lover*, though we pointed to its effect of building up suspense in our return to the poem early in this chapter. Little, indeed, needs to be said about metre in connection with a ballad, beyond the fact that it is the beat of the melody to which the words are to be *sung*. It is not used, as Donne uses it, to control the way in which the words are to be *spoken*.

Let us now return to our run-on line:

> Despair behind, and death before doth cast
> Such terror,

We agreed that it would be unthinkably silly to make a long pause after 'cast', as that reduces the sentence to nonsense. We agreed further that, while a reading of the words without the slightest pause after 'cast' would not destroy their sense, it would mean that we were turning Donne's verse into prose. In slurring one line into the next, we would be deliberately ignoring the fact that the line, from the point of view of metre, is a complete whole, a complete series of five feet:

> Despair | behind, | and death | before | doth cast

124

You may argue that the only way to bring this out when reading the line aloud is to treat it as an end-stopped line, a treatment we have rejected as ridiculous. But it is not necessary to do anything of the sort. The correct reading of the line is midway between the two extremes. We must make a pause, though only a very short one, after 'cast', because it is the end of the line, the end of a complete series of feet. The end of a line is, after all, the end of the line, and there must be some kind of break to show that it *is* the end of the line. But the break in this example cannot be a long and decided one; and, above all, the pitch of the voice must be kept up, just as though there were no pause after 'cast' at all. So the correct reading would go something like this: 'Despair behind, and death before doth cast— such terror'. The voice is kept up on 'cast', there is a moment's hesitation, and then we come down on the words 'Such terror'. Donne has made the sense run on from one line into the next because he wants a particular effect produced by the break between 'cast' and 'Such terror'.

Before we describe this particular effect, we must consider an additional reason why we have to pause after 'cast'. This poem differs from a passage of prose not only in that it uses metre, but in that it uses *rhyme*.

A very great deal of the finest poetry makes no use of rhyme at all, as the passage from Milton on p. 150 shows. When it is used, it may have various functions. In a ballad like *The Demon Lover*, rhyme does no more than produce a pleasant effect on the ear, highly suitable for a poem intended to be sung. Much poetry employs rhyme in the same way. There is nothing at all to be said against it. But a great poet will often use rhyme in quite a different way, as Donne has used it here. 'Cast' rhymes with 'fast', in the third line of the poem. Once again we must assume that Donne knew what he was doing. If he used rhyme, he used it deliberately, and if he used it deliberately he intended his rhymes to be *heard*. When a rhyme comes at the close of an end-stopped line, the reader cannot help bringing it out properly. Look at 'yesterday' in the fourth line, and 'way' in the fifth, which rhyme with 'decay' in the first line as well as with one another. But what do we do with a rhyme coming at the end of a run-on line?

The answer is that as the rhyme is meant to be heard, the reader must linger over it sufficiently for it to make its effect. This does not mean absurdly *dragging* it out—'ca-a-a-a-ast'—but merely 'leaning' on the rhyming sound, so that it is adequately brought out, without being exaggerated. Once more, the voice must be kept up, as the sense is not yet complete. Needless to say, the reading 'Despair behind, and death before doth cast such terror', entirely ignores the rhyme.

Thus we have two reasons for not turning Donne's verse into prose. We must treat the line-ending *as* a line-ending, and we must ensure that 'cast' is properly brought out as a rhyme-word: 'Despair behind, and death before doth cast (gently leaning on the word)— such terror'.

Now we are in a position to describe the particular effect Donne obtains by doing all this. Consider the meaning of the words. Whichever way he looks, he is sure to see something terrifying. Terror is what dominates him at this point. And when we ask ourselves why his terror comes across to us so vividly, we realize that it has a lot to do with the pause after 'cast'. Notice what happens during that pause, for it is not an empty one. The natural thing to do is to take a quick breath before 'Such terror'. It is here, in this intake of breath, that we have the main explanation of our sense of overwhelming terror. For what else does it suggest if not a gasp of fear, fear so great that the words 'Such terror' will not come from the lips at once? And observe that, when they do come, the fact that there has been a pause makes 'terror' vibrate with a kind of shuddering emphasis: 'Such *terror*'.

This discussion may have struck you as unduly long. It will not, however, be necessary to go through it all again when we meet similar effects in this poem and, later on, in other poems by different men living in different periods. We have examined in detail the working of one important poetic device. On the one hand there is what we call the *verse-structure*—the arrangement of the words into lines based upon a certain metre. On the other hand there is the flow of the *sense*. The verse-structure calls for a pause at the end of the line, particularly because a rhyme-word is involved, but the sense goes on without a break. Donne has exploited this situation in order to obtain one correct reading of his words. This particular reading has been obtained by the device of *playing off the sense against the verse-structure*. It is in those words that I shall speak of the device when we come across further examples of its use.

We need not go far to find the next instance:

> and my feeble flesh doth waste
> By sin in it, which it t'wards hell doth weigh.

Again the sense runs on; again the line—that is, the first line—ends with a rhyme word. There is a moment's agonized pause before the word 'sin', which comes out with terrible emphasis, an emphasis which would be nothing like so powerful without that brief hesitation after 'waste'.

We have already observed that the movement at the beginning of this group of lines seems heavily weighed down, and that when we come to the word 'weigh' we realize just how appropriate this is. But the movement is not slow and heavy only at the beginning. Consider what one has to do in order clearly to articulate the words 'sin in it'. It would be almost as easy to say those words quickly one after the other as it would be to say 'dimeyes'. And it would sound even more absurd: 'sininit'! The fact that the same vowel sound occurs in each word makes it necessary for the reader to detach the words from one another with great care, if they are to sound intelligible instead of being a meaningless jumble. This of course makes the words move slowly, deliberately, and heavily. The verse really does seem to be weighed down by a burden. Finally, notice how the voice drops on the word 'weigh', coming as it does at the conclusion of the octave (the first eight lines). The sinking effect is given additional weight by the heavily emphasized rhyme—heavily emphasized because 'weigh' rhymes with *three* previous words. Thus Donne's feeling of being weighed down towards hell by a burden of deadly sin is enacted by the movement itself.

With the opening of the sestet, the feeling changes. If the octave seems heavily to sink to its close, the sestet begins with quite the opposite effect. Instead of the '*downward*' impressions produced by 'hell' and 'weigh', we have the '*upward*' effect of 'above' and 'rise', together with the traditional notion of heaven, towards which the poet now looks, being 'above'. The movement, too, is for the most part rapid and easy, suggesting a wonderful recovery of hope and vigour. Even though Donne feels himself to be near to physical extinction, his spirit seems suddenly to have taken on a new lease of life.

I said that the movement here is *for the most part* rapid and easy, because there is one important place in which it is not. It is quite easy to say 'Only thou art above', or 'and when towards thee'; easier still to say 'I rise again'. But we have to make a definite effort to get our tongues round the words 'By thy leave I can look'. In these words the movement is very considerably slowed down. Why has the poet done this? What can be his reason for retarding the movement at this point? Let us again take it for granted that Donne knew what he was doing, and look to the meaning of the lines for an explanation. We have said that there is in these lines a wonderful sense of hope and relief. It springs from the poet's awareness that God can still help him to repent, however great the burden of sin he bears. Turning towards God, he feels that he is indeed rising again. But at the same time he knows that he, sinner as he is, can look towards God only because God mercifully permits him to do so, only because God graciously gives him 'leave'. This he must never allow himself to forget. It is when he reminds us of this that the poet checks for a moment the hopeful, springing movement. It is a moment of sober reflection. Renewed hope there certainly is, but Donne must not let it run away with him. So he pulls himself up momentarily, remembering that even the possibility of hope itself rests with God; and he pulls up the movement of the verse at the same time.

The renewed hope is in any case short-lived. No sooner are the two lines over than there comes a return of fear and gloom:

> But our old subtle foe so tempteth me,
> That not one hour my self I can sustain;

'Our old subtle foe' is obviously Satan. As for the temptation with which he plagues Donne, it must be the temptation to lapse into despair—despair that his sins are too great for God's forgiveness. This was itself a sin of unbelief. Yet he has not actually given way to this temptation, strong though it is. He is agonizingly aware of it; aware, too, that he is unable to resist it on his own, even for one hour. How can he find a way out of this situation?

The answer comes in the last two lines:

> Thy Grace may wing me to prevent his art,
> And thou like Adamant draw mine iron heart.

There is one thing, and one thing only, that he can do—put himself in the hands of God for sustenance to repent and overcome temptation. A good dictionary comes in handy at this point. It is not hard to see the general meaning of the lines: only the grace of God may give the poet 'wings' to fly from the subtle, artful temptation of Satan; and God may draw to himself the hard heart of the sinner. But we cannot appreciate the full force of the words until we know their precise meaning.

There are two words here used in senses unfamiliar to people who are acquainted with English only as it is spoken and written today. To find out what they meant at the time of Donne is a perfectly legitimate and quite simple piece of 'background' exploration. The first word is 'prevent'. Perhaps it would not be quite accurate to say that this word, as used today, has lost its old meaning. Nowadays we almost always use the word in some such expression as 'to prevent an accident'. However, consider what that expression means. When we prevent an accident, we do something to stop the accident taking place. And we are able to do this because we foresee the possibility of an accident and act in anticipation of it. We *forestall* the accident;

we do something *before* it has a full chance of occurring. Or take the expression 'Prevention is better than cure'. It is better to do something to guard yourself against catching a sickness *before* it has the opportunity to attack you than to cure it once you have already fallen a victim to it. In fact, the old meaning of 'to prevent' was simply 'to go before', and this meant that the word could be used in a wider range of contexts than those familiar today. The present-day meaning does not make nonsense in Donne's poem: the grace of God may help Donne to put a stop to the 'art' of Satan, or at any rate to stop it having any effect on him. But obviously this cannot be the complete meaning, for how can Donne put a stop to temptation by being given wings? Plainly, 'to prevent his art' must mean 'to go *before* his art', to be always in advance of Satan so that he cannot catch the poet unawares. And this fits in perfectly with the idea of God's grace giving him wings. With wings he can always 'go before' the temptations of Satan, because they give him the speed to fly from them and the lightness to rise above them.

The other word we must look at is 'Adamant'. In this case the meaning of the word as used today just will not do. For one thing, we use the word nowadays as an adjective, whereas Donne uses it as a noun. 'I assure you that with regard to this matter I am adamant' is an example of the sort of context in which we are likely to find the word today, meaning 'I assure you that with regard to this matter I cannot be moved from my position, I am utterly determined to stick to my point of view in the face of all opposition'. This is easily seen to be linked up with the old use of the word as a noun, meaning an exceedingly hard, unbreakable, unyielding stone or metal. But this meaning will not fit into the context of Donne's poem. How can even the very hardest and strongest stone or metal *draw* an '*iron* heart'? Surely only a magnet can do that. And, as the Shorter Oxford English Dictionary will tell you, the word 'adamant' did once mean 'magnet'.

There remain two matters to be discussed. The first of them takes us back to the subject of *metre*. As we observed earlier, the metre upon which this poem is based is the iambic pentameter. I stress the word 'based', because the words are not slavishly tied to the metre. The iambic pentameter, we recall, is made up of five 'feet', each consisting of an unstressed syllable followed by a stressed one: ∪ – | ∪ – | ∪ – | ∪ – | ∪ –. Some lines of the poem show this pattern very closely, as we have seen:

$$\overset{\cup}{\text{Re}}\overset{–}{\text{pair}} \mid \overset{\cup}{\text{me}} \overset{–}{\text{now,}} \mid \overset{\cup}{\text{for}} \overset{–}{\text{now}} \mid \overset{\cup}{\text{mine}} \overset{–}{\text{end}} \mid \overset{\cup}{\text{doth}} \overset{–}{\text{haste,}}$$

The pattern is clearly revealed in that line because we *naturally* stress the words in just that way when we are reading them aloud. There is no other way of reading them. We would stress them in exactly the same manner even if they occurred in a piece of prose. Imagine the absurdity of trying to stress them differently: 'REpair ME now, FOR now MINE end DOTH haste'. Our ordinary sense of how words are spoken does not permit such a ridiculous and unnatural reading.

We give a name to the way in which we stress words according to our common, everyday sense of how they must be said. It is called 'speech rhythm'. The word 'rhythm' itself is very often misunderstood. Many people confuse it with metre. In point of fact, rhythm can exist without any metre at all. Everything a person says, everything a person writes, possesses *rhythm*. Take the sentence 'I ran down the road'. Can we say that in a dead, level way, giving precisely the same emphasis to each word? Of course not. The natural speech rhythm, into which we instinctively fall when we say the words, is 'I *ran down* the *road*'. The rhythm could be different only if the person speaking wanted to make it clear that *he*, as distinct from someone else, had run down the road, or that it was the road, rather than some other place, down which he had run. In that case '*I*' or '*road*' respectively would be powerfully stressed. So speech rhythm is determined partly by our everyday sense of how words are said, and partly by the particular shade of meaning the speaker wishes to convey.

In the line 'Repair me now, for now mine end doth haste', it

131   5-2

happens that the speech rhythm of the words, and the metre in which they are arranged, exactly fit one another. To put it more succinctly, they *coincide*. It is because speech rhythm and metre coincide in quite a deal of well-known poetry that so many people think that rhythm and metre are the same thing. They coincide in Gray's famous *Elegy*, for instance:

The curfew tolls the knell of parting day.

But what happens in the opening lines of Donne's sonnet? Do speech rhythm and metre coincide here?

Thou hast made me, and shall thy work decay?

There would seem at first to be no difficulty about the second half of the line. We quite naturally put stress on 'shall', 'work', and the second syllable of 'decay'. But in the first half of the line speech rhythm and metre definitely do not coincide. According to the metre, only the words 'hast' and 'me' should be stressed, which would produce the grossly unnatural reading 'Thou HAST made ME'. Our sense of how they ought to be spoken leads us naturally to stress *each one* of the words, with an additionally heavy emphasis, as we observed earlier, on 'made'. And 'made', if we look only at the metre, is not supposed to be stressed at all!

With this in mind, we may now be struck by the fact that even the second half of the line is not quite as regular as we had imagined it to be. Stresses certainly do occur on the words we have already referred to, but the sense of the words seems to make one more stress inevitable—on 'thy'. The poet is emphasizing the fact that he has been made by *God*; he is *God's* work. Thus we have one more example of a stress falling in a manner which contradicts the strict beat of the metre.

In the line 'I run to death, and death meets me as fast', speech rhythm and metre *almost* exactly coincide. There is just one place where the stresses in the metre do not satisfy our sense of how the words should 'go'. The metre, in the second half of the line, would have us stress the words 'death', 'me', and 'fast'. These stresses, we feel, come in precisely the right places. Our only quarrel with the metre is that it invites us to treat 'meets' as an unstressed word, which would mean giving it no more emphasis than 'and' or 'as'. We could in fact treat it like that without being grossly absurd: 'and DEATH meets ME as FAST'. Yet we cannot escape from our sense that it is natural to stress all three words, 'death meets me', even though we feel that 'me' requires slightly more weight than the others: 'and DEATH MEETS ME as FAST'. The reader might try going through the whole poem, looking for places where speech rhythm and metre exactly coincide, where they are at odds with one another, and where they coincide almost but not quite.

Thus we see that Donne, in addition to playing off the sense against the verse-structure from time to time, often plays off speech rhythm against metre. The most immediate effect of this device is variety. Words are heavily weighted where the metre would lead us to expect a weak accent, and vice versa. But that is by no means the most important of the effects this device can produce. Much more fundamental is the impression given by it of absolute natural-ness, of listening to a man speaking as though he were a character in a play being performed on the stage. This remark needs qualifi-cation in two ways. 'Absolute naturalness' must on no account be taken to imply anything in the nature of *relaxation*. The reader does not simply gratefully abandon himself to the flow of the verse, as though all the work were being done for him. On the contrary, the constant need to play off speech rhythm against metre in one's reading produces a powerful drive, and a sense of being positively forced through something. Again, if the poem gives one the im-pression of a man speaking, it is because the reader, attending to the sense and movement of the words, feels *himself* to be speaking the words, whether he actually utters them aloud or not. It would be an exaggeration to say that we forget, as we listen, that this is poetry; yet to make such a remark does perhaps suggest the overall effect of Donne's sonnet. This, we feel, is the impassioned speech of a man going through an intense emotional experience. And yet this powerful, dramatic impression of an actual speaking voice, this effect of absolute naturalness, is the result of the most highly conscious *art*. It has taken all Donne's genius in the handling of rhythm, metre, and movement, to make us feel that this, and this only, is the way in which a man undergoing such an experience must speak.

In *The Demon Lover*, speech rhythm and metre nearly always exactly coincide. Once again, the simple reason for this is that a ballad is a song, each stanza being sung to the same tune. It follows that the stressed words and syllables must coincide with the stressed beats in the tune, and since the tune remains the same throughout the ballad, the verbal stresses must come in the same places from stanza to stanza, with only the tiniest room for variation here and there. There is, of course, a great deal of poetry *not* meant to be sung, in which speech rhythm and metre coincide. Gray's *Elegy* is one example we have mentioned, and we shall find other instances among the poems to be discussed in the next chapter. Poetry of this kind is neither inferior nor superior to 'Thou hast made me'—at any rate, not for that reason. There are many ways in which the human voice may speak, and for some poets in some periods the effect of naturalness is caught by a high degree of coincidence between speech rhythm and metre. A great poet's handling of his art depends always upon what he has to say.

The other subject which should be briefly considered at this point—briefly, because it will come up in connection with every poem discussed in our final chapter—is the question of *imagery*. We had occasion to touch on this matter when examining Dickens's presentation of the Smallweed family—a passage of prose which in many ways can be called 'poetic', so consciously does it exploit the suggestive possibilities of language. In that passage, we pointed to a *simile* and a *metaphor*. We can easily find both types of image in 'Thou hast made me'. The last line of the poem conveniently gives us an example of a simile—'thou *like Adamant*', and a metaphor—'draw mine *iron heart*'. But similes and metaphors, together with the other types of imagery familiar from the class-room and the text-book, do not exhaust the topic. Effects generated by *movement* may be classed as a type of imagery. The kind of *enactment* of the meaning by the movement of the verse, already pointed out in this poem, can be put under this head:

> and my feeble flesh doth waste
> By sin in it, which it t'wards hell doth weigh;

To conclude this chapter, one extremely common mistake regarding imagery must be disposed of once and for all. This is the notion that imagery must be *visual*. The idea arises from the word 'image' in its quite different meaning of a 'pictorial representation'. However, though imagery can be visual, either in part or in whole, the proper association of the word is not with pictures but with the word 'imagination'. Imagery is something bodied forth by the writer's *imagination*. In a metaphor, two or more things, not normally thought of as being connected with each other, are brought together and fused into one in the imagination of the literary artist. It is the writer's imagination which catches at hitherto unperceived relations between things; and contact with the workings of a great writer's imagination can thus give us a completely new and refreshing sense of the world in which we live.

7. POETS IN PERSPECTIVE

It is not the object of this chapter to give a miniature history of English poetry. A recital of names and dates would have little to do with our central concern—understanding literature. The poems chosen for discussion are arranged, however, in order of centuries, so as to give some idea of the outline of the English poetic tradition.

Discussion of them, for the most part, will be brief, and will not aim at exhaustiveness. Such things as classical references will be left to the reader to look up for himself; and also the reference to a Shakespeare sonnet in the poem from Eliot's *Ash Wednesday*. It is hoped that the reader, through having his attention drawn to a few of the most interesting points in each poem, will feel urged to proceed with the business of complete analysis on his own, perhaps taking our treatment of Donne's sonnet as a guide.

We shall not in every case discuss an entire poem, as some poets only reveal their true characteristics in works of great or at any rate considerable length. From such works we shall select extracts, hoping that the reader will at some time make a point of relating each passage to its context.

THE SIXTEENTH CENTURY

The stanzas below are taken from a poem called *Prothalamion*, written in the year 1596 to celebrate the double marriage of two noble couples. The spelling has here been almost entirely modernized, though certain typographical peculiarities, like the use of capital letters for some non-proper nouns, have been retained.

> There, in a Meadow, by the River's side,
> A Flock of *Nymphs* I chanced to espy,
> All lovely daughters of the Flood thereby,
> With goodly greenish locks all loose untied,
> As each had been a Bride,

And each one had a little wicker basket,
Made of fine twigs entrailed curiously,
In which they gathered flowers to fill their flasket:
And with fine Fingers, cropped full feateously
The tender stalks on high.
Of every sort, which in that Meadow grew,
They gathered some; the Violet pallid blue,
The little Daisie, that at evening closes,
The virgin Lily, and the Primrose true,
With store of vermeil Roses,
To deck their Bridegrooms' posies,
Against the Bridal day, which was not long:
 Sweet *Thames* run softly, till I end my Song.

With that, I saw two Swans of goodly hue,
Come softly swimming down along the Lea;
Two fairer birds I yet did never see:
The snow which doth the top of *Pindus* strew,
Did never whiter shew,
Nor *Jove* himself when he a Swan would be
For love of *Leda*, whiter did appear:
Yet *Leda* was they say as white as he,
Yet not so white as these, nor nothing near;
So purely white they were,
That even the gentle stream, the which them bare,
Seem'd foul to them, and bade his billows spare
To wet their silken feathers, lest they might
Soil their fair plumes with water not so fair,
And mar their beauties bright,
That shone as heaven's light,
Against their Bridal day, which was not long:
 Sweet *Thames* run softly, till I end my Song.

EDMUND SPENSER

What are the most striking features of these stanzas? Perhaps the
best way to approach an answer is to say first of all that they are
clearly quite unlike anything in either *The Demon Lover* or 'Thou
hast made me'. Instead of the fast-moving narrative of the ballad,
with its strict economy and vividly abrupt transitions, there is a sense
of leisurely expansiveness. The first of the two stanzas concerns
'A Flock of *Nymphs*' in a riverside meadow, the second 'two Swans

of Goodly hue'. There is absolutely no feeling of narrative urgency in the way the poet tells us about these sights. In this case it is genuinely appropriate to say that the poetry has a visual appeal, as it is the *appearance* of the nymphs and the swans that really interests Spenser. He is setting out to surround them with an atmosphere of the utmost delicacy and freshness, and he is in no hurry about it, preferring rather to linger over every lovely detail so delightedly conjured up by his imagination.

A helpful way of looking at these stanzas is to liken them to a gorgeous piece of elaborate weaving or embroidery. The first one gives us a luxuriant floral design, while the second presents to the mental eye a ravishing picture of the superlative whiteness and exquisite texture of the swans' plumage. Indeed, it may already have struck the reader that the effect of this poetry is essentially *decorative*. Little seems actually to be *said* in either stanza. What we have is rather the decorative elaboration of two basic ideas. In the first stanza, the centre of interest, which provides the excuse for a verbal equivalent of floral decorations, is the contents of the 'little wicker basket' carried by each nymph. In the second, the fanciful scheme is simply a way of decoratively spinning out the fact that the swans were of a whiteness never previously beheld by the poet, and perhaps never previously beheld by anyone at all. The references to '*Pindus*', and to the story of Leda and the Swan (a classical dictionary should be consulted here), are, strictly speaking, irrelevant; but they are brought in to enhance the general tapestry-like effect.

If we think back to the manner in which John Donne uses verse in 'Thou hast made me', we shall realize that Spenser is using it in a completely different spirit. The clue to the difference is in the last line of each stanza:

> Sweet *Thames* run softly, till I end my Song.

Prothalamion is not a 'Song', but there is undeniably a quality in the poem that tempts us to call it 'song-like'. The reader will probably have been told at some time or other that one of the chief beauties of poetry is its 'musical' quality, and may well have been encouraged to applaud poetry which obviously possesses this quality, to the detriment of poetry which does not. Now, whatever may happen in other kinds of poetry, Spenser is here exploring musical possibilities of a rather simple kind. 'Musical' must not, of course, be taken literally. The words do not affect the reader or listener by virtue of their sound alone. If their sound does here produce what we may call a musical effect, their meaning and associations have a very great deal to do with the phenomenon.

Nevertheless, Spenser is very much concerned with the sound-patterns made by his words, though these sound-patterns would not exist if the words did not mean anything. Consider, for example, these lines from the first of the stanzas:

> And each one held a little wicker basket,
> Made of fine twigs entrailed curiously,
> In which they gathered flowers to fill their flasket:
> And with fine Fingers, cropped full feateously
> The tender stalks on high.

Notice the alliteration in the third and fourth lines, and the deft manner in which Spenser, after four lines each consisting of five feet—though 'basket' and 'flasket', by unobtrusively slipping in an extra syllable, almost have the effect of introducing an extra foot—varies the rhythm by slipping in one of three. But these devices can hardly be said to drive home, or be dictated by, any pressure in the poet's overall meaning. When Donne varies his rhythms—though in the sonnet we examined he does not vary his line lengths and consequently his metre—he does so because the pressure of what he has to say inescapably forces him to do it. Again, his use of alliteration is quite different from Spenser's:

> I dare not move my dim eyes any way,
> Despair behind, and death before doth cast
> Such terror,

The alliteration here powerfully contributes to our sense of the urgency of the situation. It is, in fact, being used *dramatically*.

With Spenser, on the other hand, there is no dramatic reason for 'fine Fingers' and 'full feateously'. Donne employs alliteration to make the reader focus attention on the situation, to make us feel, because the words are associated alliteratively, that the facts that he does not 'dare', that his eyes are 'dim', that 'Despair' and 'death' fill him with overmastering terror, are part and parcel of the one appalling situation; whereas Spenser uses the device merely to charm the ear.

The word 'musical' may also be applied, in a different sense, to the way in which the second quoted stanza is put together. Here we have something that can be likened to a rising and falling melodic line. The stanza opens quietly and calmly enough. The swans are described merely as being 'of goodly hue', and they are swimming 'softly'. With the downright and perhaps extravagant declaration of the third line, a certain quickening of the pulse is felt; and through the next six lines, with their insistence on the words 'white' and 'whiter', the 'melody' soars, reaching a climax in 'So purely white they were'—which, however, because the line is shorter than its immediate predecessors, brings about at its end a relaxation and a falling of the melody, which revives momentarily in 'that shone as heaven's light' and then sinks quietly to the refrain, which echoes the 'softly' of the second line.

More light can be thrown on the musical quality of these stanzas by setting representative lines of Donne and Spenser side by side:

> I dare not move my dim eyes any way,
> Despair behind, and death before doth cast
> Such terror,

> There, in a Meadow, by the River's side,
> A Flock of *Nymphs* I chanced to espy,
> All lovely daughters of the Flood thereby,
> With goodly greenish locks all loose untied,
> As each had been a Bride,

What is the essential difference between these examples? The answer is that Spenser's lines, when read aloud, move very much more smoothly and easily than Donne's. By comparison with Spenser, Donne seems almost rough and uncouth. There is nothing in the fragment from Spenser which has the clogged, laboured effect of 'I dare not move my dim eyes any way'. Ease and difficulty of articulation do vary from place to place in Spenser's stanzas, but the *predominant* impression is that of ease.

It used to be commonly said that Donne's verse was defective because of its harshness and ruggedness. The only sensible comment to make on such a view is that if his verse is indeed harsh and rugged, it is harsh and rugged with the harshness and ruggedness of human speech. Anyone who supposes that Donne's verse is incompetent because it lacks the smoothness of Spenser's, should remind himself of the careful way in which the former poet has handled his verse-structure in order to catch the tones of the passionate speaking voice of a man in terror of imminent damnation. If the movement of the verse stumbles from time to time, if it is often impeded, if it seems full of jolts and jars, it is because the poet needs these effects in order to convey his meaning, because of the very harshness of what he has to say. Indeed, one can go further, and say that these effects are actually *part of the meaning*.

Spenser, by contrast, handles his language in such a way that the jolts and jars to which English is prone are reduced to a minimum. They are 'ironed out', as it were. To say this does not mean that he is a more skilful poet than Donne, but that his undertaking is of a completely different kind. Donne wishes to obtain an effect of the utmost urgency and immediacy, while Spenser progresses in a leisurely fashion, unfolding in easily moving verse a rich design of visual impressions and an exquisite fabric of verbal music. There is hardly a trace of the visual in Donne's sonnet. He wishes us to feel the urgency of the situation in our very nerves, not to paint pictures in the mind's eye. To make us do this, he uses his verse to enact the meaning in its actual movement. Spenser does not handle his verse in that way at all. The only possible exception to this is the effect produced by the refrain, where it might be said that the soft flowing of the river is suggested by the smoothness of the movement.

Nothing, indeed, could be more characteristically Spenserian than these stanzas, and consideration of them takes one beyond Spenser alone. Spenser had an enormous influence upon subsequent poets. He might be described as the poetic 'reservoir' from which Milton, a host of eighteenth-century poets who imitated Milton, and later Keats and Tennyson, drew many of their effects. In the first of the stanzas there is the floral imagery which Milton uses copiously in much of his minor poetry, and which Keats revived—though not in such poems as the Ode we are later to examine; and the art exemplified in the 'melodic' structure of the second stanza leads straight to the art of 'sustaining a period' displayed by Milton and Tennyson.

It is not hard to see why Donne and Spenser are so different. To produce an effect of the immediacy we find in Donne's sonnet would destroy the serenity and thus be fatal to Spenser's purpose.

THE SEVENTEENTH CENTURY

To his Coy Mistress

Had we but world enough and time,
This coyness, lady, were no crime.
We would sit down and think which way
To walk, and pass our long love's day.
Thou by the Indian Ganges' side
Shouldst rubies find: I by the tide
Of Humber would complain. I would
Love you ten years before the Flood,
And you should, if you please, refuse
Till the conversion of the Jews.
My vegetable love should grow
Vaster than empires and more slow.
An hundred years should go to praise
Thine eyes, and on thy forehead gaze;
Two hundred to adore each breast,
But thirty thousand to the rest;

An age at least to every part,
And the last age should show your heart.
For, lady, you deserve this state,
Nor would I love at lower rate.
But at my back I always hear
Time's winged chariot hurrying near,
And yonder all before us lie
Deserts of vast eternity.
Thy beauty shall no more be found,
Nor in thy marble vault shall sound
My echoing song; then worms shall try
That long-preserved virginity,
And your quaint honour turn to dust,
And into ashes all my lust.
The grave's a fine and private place,
But none, I think, do there embrace.
Now, therefore, while the youthful hue
Sits on thy skin like morning dew,
And while thy willing soul transpires
At every pore with instant fires,
Now, let us sport us while we may;
And now, like amorous birds of prey,
Rather at once our time devour,
Than languish in his slow-chapt power!
Let us roll all our strength, and all
Our sweetness up into one ball;
And tear our pleasures with rough strife,
Thorough the iron gates of life!
Thus, though we cannot make our sun
Stand still, yet we will make him run.

ANDREW MARVELL

The theme of this poem is the age-old idea that since life does not last for ever, one should take full advantage of it while it is still in one's possession. In this particular instance, the poet is calling upon his mistress, who has been bashfully withholding herself, to overcome her coyness and yield to his entreaties. If they had unlimited time at their disposal, this coyness would not matter. But time is always passing, and the danger is that death may overtake them before they have had the chance to come together. So the poet urges her to join with him in a challenge to time. They cannot prevent its passing, but in the enjoyment of their mutual love they can use what little time they have to the full.

To his Coy Mistress will probably strike the reader as not being at all 'poetic' in the Spenserian manner. In fact he may think that one may hardly apply the word 'poetic' to it in any way. Perhaps he will make an exception of four lines:

> But at my back I always hear
> Time's winged chariot hurrying near,
> And yonder all before us lie
> Deserts of vast eternity.

He may say that those lines are 'poetic' because they are solemn, whereas the rest of the thing has a disconcerting way of deviating into a kind of flippancy that we do not normally expect of poetry. But may one ask him why flippancy—if indeed that is actually what we find here—should not at times be a legitimate ingredient of poetry? His reply to that will probably be that poetry ought to be 'serious', and that whatever takes away from seriousness must be anti-poetic. If by 'seriousness', however, he means 'solemnity', as he almost certainly does, may one go on to suggest that they are by no means inevitably the same thing?

To his Coy Mistress is a serious poem, but its kind of seriousness does not exclude humour and even downright levity. It is the seriousness of an adult mind, a mind which knows that human life is a complex affair, and that there are many different angles from which a given situation may be viewed. Reading the poem is likewise a complex business. We must be prepared for sharp transitions from one point of view to another, showing themselves in alterations of *tone*. 'Tone' is not a difficult word to understand in relation to poetry. It means neither more nor less than the tone of voice one would imagine the poet to adopt were he speaking the words aloud himself.

Now, the tone in the first eighteen lines of the poem, if they were taken by themselves, might very well suggest that Marvell is not being serious. What he gives is a catalogue of impossibilities—things he and his mistress would be able to do if only they had 'world enough and time', which almost amounts to having eternity. He knows that these things are absurdly out of the question, so he has no scruple in making each idea a monument of extravagance. Notice how this is brought out in the tone, and observe how the tone is often controlled by the way in which the verse is handled. There is a good example of this here:

> I would
> Love you ten years before the Flood,

Having 'world enough and time' apparently means going back to a period long before one's own life began! And the absurdity of the whole notion is brought out by the pause, though the voice is kept up, after 'would'. There is a moment's hesitation, we wonder what is coming, and then the preposterous idea is announced. Another instance of Marvell's control of tone through the handling of verse-structure may be drawn from this opening section:

> My vegetable love should grow
> Vaster than empires and more slow.

Here the pause at the end of the run-on line leads to a heavy stress on 'Vaster', and once again reinforces our sense of the sheer extravagance of what is being said. We can almost imagine the poet opening his arms wide in comic demonstration of his words— '*Vast*er than *emp*ires...'. The reader should look for further instances of this kind of effect in the first twenty lines.

For eighteen lines, then, the poet is plainly not being serious in any commonly understood sense of that word. He would be prepared to let his mistress wander by the side of the Ganges in India whilst he moped by the banks of the River Humber in England. He would be happy to spend a vast succession of years in the adoration of each of her beauties. All this, needless to say, had they 'but world enough and time', which of course they have not! The list of impossibilities is so fantastic that one wonders whether or not the poet really means what he says in praise of the lady. Is he really paying her a magnificent compliment by means of all this extravagance, or is he simply indulging in a huge joke, an idle piece of flirtatious gallantry?

Our doubts might at first seem to be resolved by the last two lines of the opening section:

> For, lady, you deserve this state,
> Nor would I love at lower rate.

The tone has certainly changed somewhat from the flippant banter of what has gone before. The poet, we feel, is speaking now with greater seriousness; he really does love and esteem the lady. Yet this is not the whole story. Although we feel that there is some difference between these lines and their predecessors, it is impossible not to feel, at the same time, that the poet's tongue is still in his cheek. After all, whatever the extent of his love and esteem for her, no lady could possibly deserve the kind of 'state' and 'rate' that have been imagined! He is sincere in his love for her, but his sincerity does not preclude a continuing note of playfulness.

None the less, the sincerity is there, and the lines provide an effective transition to what follows. In them the banter of the opening is blended with a hint of seriousness which the element of sincerity brings in. This is how he *would* love her, if only time permitted, because he feels that she merits all the love and praise that 'world enough and time' could allow him to bestow upon her.

For the first time we feel that Marvell is being, in quite an ordinary sense, 'serious'. He means what he says; he is not simply playing the fool, as we may have suspected. This seriousness introduces a sober note, which prepares us for the impressive 'solemnity' of the next four lines:

> But at my back I always hear
> Time's winged chariot hurrying near,
> And yonder all before us lie
> Deserts of vast eternity.

146

Time is always catching up, and the eternity which faces the poet and his mistress is not an eternity in which he can love and praise her, but the 'vast eternity' that stretches after death. The nature of this eternity, so very different from the near-eternity extravagantly conjured up in the first section, is superbly suggested by the word 'Deserts', which is placed in the verse-structure with absolute mastery. There is a catch of the breath after 'lie', then the stress comes down on 'Deserts' with an effect of awe and dread. This 'vast eternity' will hold, not opportunities for almost endless pro-crastination, but mere sterile emptiness.

The solemnity continues through the next two lines and a half:

> Thy beauty shall no more be found,
> Nor in thy marble vault shall sound
> My echoing song.

Part of the effect of these lines is an impression of chill desolation, produced by the idea of the lady's death and burial brought in by the word 'vault', and by the associations of sepulchral coldness going with 'marble'. Added to this is the idea of the poet's song 'echoing' round the emptiness of the lady's vault. It is true that Marvell says his song will *not* be heard there; but the use of 'echoing' makes us for a moment imagine it eerily sounding in the cold and empty place.

It would be a mistake, however, to put too much stress, or the wrong kind of stress, on all this. For one thing, the eeriness is qualified by our reflection that the notion of singing in a 'marble vault' is a somewhat ludicrous one, and that it is partly meant to be taken as such. Indeed, if we are reading attentively, it is prac-tically impossible to attach too much importance to the 'solemnity'. The poet *is* aware that time passes swiftly and that death is inevitable, but we have all the time to remember that his insistence on these things is part of a plan of campaign, the object of which is to make the lady yield to him. Our consciousness of his basic intention must prevent us from taking him too seriously. The solemnity is certainly there, but there is a generous admixture of irony.

In the lines which follow, the irony is overt:

> then worms shall try
> That long-preserved virginity,
> And your quaint honour turn to dust,
> And into ashes all my lust.

The gruesome thought of the dissolution of the body after death is made a means of poking fun at the lady. If she preserves her virginity indefinitely in life, the worms will make short work of it once she is dead! Where will be the point of her 'honour' then? And this mockery leads to the plain outrageousness of the last two lines of this section, which recall, in a different context, the levity of the opening:

> The grave's a fine and private place,
> But none, I think, do there embrace.

In the last section the word 'Now' is placed so as to receive maximum stress:

> *Now*, therefore,...
> *Now*, let us sport us while we may;
> And *now*, like amorous birds of prey,....

It is as though Marvell were saying 'Let us delay no longer. We know we cannot live for ever. Let us therefore take full advantage of life while we still have it, NOW! Instead of being the victims of time, and allowing "him" to devour us in his slowly moving jaws, let us rather devour *our* time, as birds of prey devour what they have caught.' Notice how the idea of the slowly moving jaws of time is enacted by the movement: 'Than languish in his slow-chapt power!' The difficulty involved in articulating the words results in a laborious slowness magnificently appropriate to the meaning. Observe, too, an example of enactment in the lines which suggest the headlong flight of a cannon-ball tearing its way through iron fortifications:

> And tear our pleasures with rough strife,
> Thorough the iron gates of life!

148

(The idea of a cannon-ball is indicated by linking the 'ball' into which the lovers should roll all their strength and sweetness with the violence of these two lines.) The words are chosen so as to give an impression of roughness when read aloud. Speech rhythm and metre are here conspicuously at variance with each other. 'Rough' and 'strife' receive the same heavy emphasis, and it is the first syllable of 'Thorough' that speech rhythm obliges us to stress.

The last two lines of the poem exhibit the same mastery of the possibilities of verse:

> Thus, though we cannot make our sun
> Stand still, yet we will make him run.

The pause at the end of the penultimate line has the effect of suggesting, for one brief moment, the idea of the sun standing still. As the run of the sense is for an instant suspended, so the sheer impossibility of time measured by the sun coming to a standstill is thought of as a possibility. The impression is intensified by the slowness imposed upon the articulation by the words 'Stand still'. But the idea is dismissed, as it has to be, and the poem ends with six defiant and quickly moving words. We can't make time come to a stop, but we can give him a good run for his money!

In the first section of the poem we have had levity finally giving way to seriousness; in the second we have moved from solemnity, through horror and mockery, to rather impudent sarcasm; and in the third we have had the tone of intense, imploring passion. The poem is not a long one, yet we have the impression, when we have finished it, of having ranged over a wide variety of feelings about the shortness of life and the implications of this for the poet and his mistress. Can we say that the effect of the poem *as a whole* is not 'serious'? To maintain that view would be to persist in an unduly limited conception of what seriousness amounts to. I have said that what we have here is the seriousness of an adult mind. Precisely. The mind is that of a man who knows life, who has his share of worldly wisdom, who knows that the most solemn topics may sometimes be seen in a humorous light. The mind is an agile and flexible one, capable of shifting from one point of view to another in an instant, yet all the while keeping a sure grasp upon the realities of the situation. We call such a mind, and the poem which has issued from it, 'sophisticated', a word that is nowadays unfortunately often badly misused. True sophistication, such as we find in this poem, is a very different thing from the expensive smartness with which the word is popularly associated today. This true sophistication is a quality found in a great deal of seventeenth-century poetry, and its mark is always the blend of ordinarily recognizable seriousness with elements which are superficially and singly far from serious, that we have met in Marvell's poem. To this blend, and to the kind of agility of thought and feeling which goes with it, we give the name '*wit*'. 'Wit', in this sense, is not to be confused with mere 'humour'. Humour will frequently enter into it, but so will vastly different ingredients. In conclusion, it seems worth saying that the experience of a large number of readers has shown poems which possess this quality to be more permanently satisfying, when constantly re-read, than many others which are more obviously 'serious' in a conventional way. Their 'wit' gives them a strength denied to poems of a relatively one-sided seriousness.

*　　*　　*

The hasty multitude
Admiring entered; and the work some praise,
And some the architect. His hand was known
In Heaven by many a towered structure high,
Where sceptred Angels held their residence,
And sat as Princes, whom the Supreme King
Exalted to such power, and gave to rule,
Each in his hierarchy, the Orders bright.
Nor was his name unheard or unadored
In ancient Greece; and in Ausonian land
Men called him Mulciber; and how he fell
From Heaven they fabled, thrown by angry Jove
Sheer o'er the crystal battlements: from morn
To noon he fell, from noon to dewy eve,
A summer's day, and with the setting sun

Dropt from the zenith, like a falling star,
On Lemnos, the Aegean isle. Thus they relate,
Erring; for he with this rebellious rout
Fell long before; nor aught availed him now
To have built in Heaven high towers; nor did he scape
By all his engines, but was headlong sent
With his industrious crew, to build in Hell.

JOHN MILTON

This passage, which comes from Book I of *Paradise Lost*, concerns the architect of Pandemonium, the splendid capital the fallen angels build for themselves in Hell. It is a fine example of Milton's blank verse at its very best, exhibiting absolute control of the possibilities of this kind of writing.

The passage falls into three fairly distinct parts, the first ending with 'Orders bright', the second with the words 'Aegean isle'. The first part tells us about Mulciber's work before his fall, while the second turns the attention to an 'Ausonian' legend about him. In the third part the legend is dismissed as fictitious, and the poet concentrates on the present situation of Mulciber, and the truth about his fall.

Milton varies his manner of handling verse from one section to another. In the first part, the verse moves slowly and majestically, almost stiffly, to accord with the stately associations of such words as 'sceptred Angels', 'sat as Princes', 'the Supreme King', 'Exalted to such power', and 'the Orders bright'. The overall effect is that of a magnificently ordered hierarchical *formality*, conveyed largely by the tendency of the principal stresses to fall regularly in much the same part of each line:

> His hand was known
> In *Heaven* by many a towered structure *high*,
> Where *sceptred Angels* held their *residence*,
> And *sat* as *Princes*, whom the Supreme *King*
> *Exalted* to such *power*, and gave to *rule*,
> *Each* in his *hierarchy*, the Orders *bright*.

In the second part of the passage there is a change. The formality disappears, and the verse begins quite suddenly to move with a new flexibility. It is as though Milton's imagination had been given wings by the thought of the Ausonian legend regarding Mulciber's fall from Heaven. Notice how his fall is enacted by the movement of the verse:

> and how he fell
> From Heaven they fabled, thrown by angry Jove
> Sheer o'er the crystal battlements:

By playing off the run of the sense against the verse-structure, the poet contrives to suggest the actual movement of falling. There is a moment of suspense after 'fell', and then the sentence tumbles, as it were, into the next line. A similar effect comes with the next line-ending. If a suitable pause is made after 'Jove', the strong emphasis on the first word in the following line, 'Sheer', gives a powerful impression of the force with which the erring Mulciber was cast out. Reading the lines aloud makes it virtually impossible to avoid *flinging* out the word: '*Sheer* o'er the crystal battlements'.

The same exploitation of verse-structure is evident in the lines which follow:

> from morn
> To noon he fell, from noon to dewy eve,
> A summer's day, and with the setting sun
> Dropt from the zenith, like a falling star,
> On Lemnos, the Aegean isle.

Here the falling of Mulciber is suggested in a particularly interesting way. The actual sense is concerned with the *time* it took him to fall from Heaven to Lemnos; yet the placing of the words in the verse-structure gives an impression of motion:

> from morn
> To *noon* he fell, from noon to dewy *eve*,
> A summer's *day*,

Again, the words 'and with the setting sun' tell us of the time of day at which Mulciber dropped on the island. But it is difficult not to associate his fall, if only for a moment, with the setting sun sinking below the horizon. Observe the perfect placing of 'Dropt', which comes out with emphatic finality as Mulciber reaches the end of his unceremonious descent.

You will perhaps have noticed that although this little story relates to a violent incident, and although much of the violence is suggested by the way in which the verse is handled, there is a curious and paradoxical atmosphere of 'glamour' about it all. Reflection shows this to be connected with certain words which have far from disagreeable associations—'crystal', 'dewy eve', 'a summer's day', 'the setting sun', 'a falling star'. Despite the powerful enactment by the verse of Mulciber's ejection and fall, the effect is rather softened by the presence of these words. It is as though the whole episode were being viewed through a romantic haze. If we want a reason for this, we shall find it in the word 'fabled'. Milton's poetic imagination may be given wings by the tale, but he does not mean to let us take it seriously. It is a mere fable, doubtless attractive, but none the less fictitious. Thus it is no accident that this section of the passage should begin and end with references to the far-off world of classical antiquity. For a few moments we are taken away from Hell and the stern realities of the fallen angels' situation, to glance briefly and may be rather nostalgically back to the Golden world of Greek legend.

The last section strikes quite a different note. Milton dismisses the Ausonian fable with a somewhat severe gesture: 'Thus they relate, *Erring*'. This version of Mulciber's fall has distracted us for a little while, he seems to be saying, but it is high time to tell what actually happened. The atmosphere of glamour accordingly disappears. No attempt is made to soften the reality—a grim reality, suggested by the studied harshness of the tone:

> for he with this rebellious rout
> Fell long before; nor aught availed him now
> To have built in Heaven high towers;

The articulation of the words gives rise to a rough and rugged movement, which continues until the speaking voice comes down with emphatic finality on the word 'Hell'. Not for Mulciber the Aegean isle. Hell is the ugly truth.

✳   ✳   ✳

Farewell, too little and too lately known,
Whom I began to think and call my own:
For sure our souls were near alli'd, and thine
Cast in the same poetic mould with mine.
One common note on either lyre did strike,
And knaves and fools we both abhorr'd alike.
To the same goal did both our studies drive:
The last set out the soonest did arrive.
Thus Nisus fell upon the slippery place,
Whilst his young friend perform'd and won the race.
O early ripe! to thy abundant store
What could advancing age have added more?
It might (what nature never gives the young)
Have taught the numbers of thy native tongue.
But satire needs not those, and wit will shine
Through the harsh cadence of a rugged line.
A noble error, and but seldom made,
When poets are by too much force betrayed.
Thy gen'rous fruits, though gather'd ere their prime,
Still show'd a quickness; and maturing time
But mellows what we write to the dull sweets of rhyme.
Once more, hail, and farewell! farewell, thou young
But ah! too short, Marcellus of our tongue!
Thy brows with ivy and with laurels bound;
But Fate and gloomy Night encompass thee around.

JOHN DRYDEN

Here we have an elegy, written *To the memory of Mr. Oldham*, himself a poet, and a young contemporary of Dryden. Just as there were probably a good many readers who felt inclined to dismiss Marvell's *To his Coy Mistress* for lack of seriousness, so there may well be some who will complain that Dryden's poem is not 'sad' enough to be a real elegy. They may feel like taking the poet to task for insincerity. From what feature of this poem could such an impression arise? Almost certainly, it has something to do with a quality—the hostile reader would call it a defect—which is perceptible immediately in the very first two lines:

> Farewell, too little and too lately known,
> Whom I began to think and call my own:

However uncongenial he may find the poem as a whole, the reader is presumably not likely to take exception to the meaning expressed here. Dryden is regretting that he knew Oldham all too little, saying that he wished they had been earlier acquainted, and that he was just beginning, when Oldham died, to regard him as being peculiarly his 'own', for reasons given in the next eight lines. If the reader does not quarrel with the meaning, then, he must be dissatisfied with its expression. Pressed to give a reason for his feeling of discomfort, he may answer that he finds the language altogether too 'neat', too 'polished', to be convincing as the expression of real sadness at the death of an admired friend.

Now, the word 'neat' is certainly not out of place in a description of these lines. They have extreme compactness and compression, as will be appreciated if they are contrasted with the explanation of their meaning given in the last paragraph. No one could deny the superiority of Dryden's precision and economy to our clumsy exposition. But perhaps the hostile reader will agree with this, while persisting in feeling that something is wrong. 'Granted that Dryden has expressed himself most concisely,' he may say, 'I still do not see what all this concern with symmetry and balance has to do with deep emotion. A man who really felt sorrow could not write like that.'

We are obliged to admit that the balance and the symmetry are there: 'Too *little*' known, on the one hand; 'too *lately* known', on the other; 'Whom I began to *think*...my own', on the one hand; 'Whom I began to...*call* my own', on the other. The same kind of thing can be readily found elsewhere in the poem: 'The *last set out*', on the one hand, 'the *soonest did arrive*', on the other. It is this prevailing sense of '*this* on the one hand, *that* on the other', which more than anything else is likely to make the reader feel uneasy. For this preoccupation with extreme pointedness of phrasing, this concern with putting precisely the right word in precisely the right place, suggests an intellectual control on the writer's part, a conscious attention to doing the job properly, which may be at odds with the reader's preconceptions regarding the correct manner in which to express personal sorrow. Yet why should this be so? Is there any reason why intellectual control and genuine emotion should not be found together? The reader who continues to feel that the two things are incompatible, should ask himself whether or not his views have been based largely on his experience of poets of the nineteenth century, and accept the possibility of revising his opinions in the light of Dryden's elegy.

This poem owes most of its distinction to a blend of intellect and emotion. The intellectual control is evident not only in the compactness of the phrasing and in the concern with symmetry; it is there also in the splendidly assured exploitation of this kind of verse, and in the judicious manner in which Oldham's own poetic achievement is critically estimated.

Consider Dryden's use of rhyme in lines three to eight. You will notice that the same 'I' sound is common to all six rhyme-words: 'thine—mine', 'strike—alike', 'drive—arrive'. This is not accidental. If you examine the meaning of the lines, you will see that their subject is the close resemblance between Dryden and his young contemporary, a likeness which leads the older poet to compare Oldham and himself to two musicians sounding 'One common note' although playing separate instruments. The use of the prevailing vowel-sound is now seen to be appropriate. The lines are bound together by this aural link, just as the two poets were bound together by their common interests and objects.

Dryden's sense of what can be done with the resources of verse is further illustrated in the lines which praise and at the same time critically qualify Oldham's achievement. He begins by asking what Oldham could have gained with 'advancing age', and suggests that possibly he might have acquired a more perfect mastery of the 'numbers' of his native tongue. That is to say, years of experience might have taught him to write English verse in a smoother and more polished manner—an accomplishment which never comes to a young poet purely as a gift of nature. But he goes on to reflect that such mastery of 'numbers' is not, after all, so very necessary for satire, and that wit will always be apparent when it is there, no matter how rough and rugged the verse may sometimes be. As if to echo his meaning, Dryden, whose own mastery of 'numbers' was consummate, purposely slips in a line whose movement actually suggests roughness: 'Through the harsh cadence of a rugged line'. Speech rhythm and metre could hardly be more at variance.

Still more can be said about Dryden's poetic felicities. A particularly grand example of what he can do with his verse is given in these lines:

> Thy gen'rous fruits, though gather'd ere their prime,
> Still show'd a quickness; and maturing time
> But mellows what we write to the dull sweets of rhyme.

Dryden is saying that although Oldham did not reach poetic maturity, his 'fruits' (i.e. his poems) possessed genuine liveliness; whereas older poets like himself do not necessarily improve with age. Advancing years, in fact, while bringing technical perfection, may bring lifelessness as well. Once again he makes his verse enact his meaning. You will have observed that the passage is unusual in that three lines are made to rhyme with one another instead of the two found everywhere else in the poem. Moreover, the third of these lines has a metrical pattern different from that of the previous ones. Instead of having five feet, it has six: 'But mel|lows what | we write | to the | dull sweets | of rhyme'. Dryden is doing two things here. He is first of all displaying his own technical skill as a user of verse—a skill which enables him to insert an extra rhyme with absolute naturalness and ease, and which permits him to introduce a line of six feet without injuring the unity of the poem. Here, to be sure, is the work of someone who has mastered the 'numbers' of his native tongue! But Dryden is also creating a deliberate impression of lifelessness. Technically masterly the lines may be. They are at the same time utterly lacking in energy. It is impossible to read the line and a half following the semi-colon with any kind of vigour. The stresses fall in a monotonous, toneless manner; there is an effect of languor and exhaustion, intensified by the extra foot. The words seem to drag themselves along with weary apathy. Thus the lines are themselves an illustration of 'the dull sweets of rhyme'. The accomplishment of the experienced poet is there for all to admire; but it is an accomplishment achieved at the expense of energy.

The reader should consult a classical dictionary to find out what the references to Nisus and Marcellus are doing in the poem. It will be found in each case that there is an implied reference to another classical figure, and that the purpose of each allusion is to emphasize the closeness of the bond between Dryden and Oldham. The whole poem is a superbly unified piece of work, in which it is at no point possible to separate Dryden's intelligence and his literary cultivation from his feeling for the dead poet. The last two lines, which even the initially hostile reader might have found convincing, are both a tender farewell and a critical tribute—a critical tribute paid by placing Oldham firmly among the laureates of classical antiquity.

THE EIGHTEENTH CENTURY

It is not easy to find an example of eighteenth-century poetry at its best which is comparable in length to the other poems and passages we have chosen for this survey. To think of the eighteenth century is to think of Pope; but most of Pope's finest work is on a large or fairly large scale, and so concentrated in its organization that it is difficult to isolate passages and expect them to be fully understood. The passage below, which is the close of his long satirical poem *The Dunciad*, has been selected with an awareness that complete comprehension of it cannot be reached until and unless the reader goes to the trouble of relating it to its context. But even if much in the passage remains obscure until the reader makes this extra effort, it should still convey something of Pope's quality.

> She comes! she comes! the sable Throne behold
> Of *Night* Primaeval, and of *Chaos* old!
> Before her, *Fancy's* gilded clouds decay,
> And all its varying Rain-bows die away.
> *Wit* shoots in vain its momentary fires,
> The meteor drops, and in a flash expires.

As one by one, at dread Medea's strain,
The sick'ning stars fade off th'ethereal plain;
As Argus' eyes by Hermes' wand opprest,
Clos'd one by one to everlasting rest;
Thus at her felt approach, and secret might,
Art after *Art* goes out, and all is Night.
See skulking *Truth* to her old Cavern fled,
Mountains of Casuistry heap'd o'er her head!
Philosophy, that lean'd on Heav'n before,
Shrinks to her second cause, and is no more.
Physic of *Metaphysic* begs defence,
And *Metaphysic* calls for aid on *Sense*!
See *Mystery* to *Mathematics* fly!
In vain! they gaze, turn giddy, rave, and die.
Religion blushing veils her sacred fires,
And unawares *Morality* expires.
Nor *public* Flame, nor *private*, dares to shine;
Nor *human* Spark is left, nor Glimpse *divine*!
Lo! thy dread Empire, CHAOS! is restor'd;
Light dies before thy uncreating word:
Thy hand, great Anarch! lets the curtain fall;
And Universal Darkness buries All.

ALEXANDER POPE

The Dunciad, which consists of four Books, is written in the outward manner of an epic poem. But instead of narrating heroic exploits, or presenting majestic visions, like a real epic, it gives a survey of the foibles, follies, and vices which Pope felt to be prevailing in the England of his time. The poem is peopled with dunces (hence the title), with the Goddess *Dulness* at their head. Every branch of life and thought becomes subject to her sway, until finally, in this closing passage, civilization dissolves into utter anarchy, and the primal chaos, traditionally thought of as existing before the Creation, is restored.

As the reader may imagine, *The Dunciad* is rich in comedy. A good deal of it needs some special acquaintance with eighteenth-century social and intellectual history to be fully appreciated, but this is not so difficult of acquisition as might be supposed, since the modern 'Twickenham' edition of the poem gives the necessary information in its notes. The effort of reading the poem at least once in that edition is well worth making.

Comedy, however, is not the sole ingredient of *The Dunciad*. By making them ridiculous Pope may condemn the follies he deplores, but the ultimate effect is far from merely laughable. Just as Marvell's *To his Coy Mistress* depends for its effect upon a blend of seriousness and light-heartedness, so Pope combines the impressive, the sensuous, and the absurd. The opening of our passage, for example, strikes a note of ominous solemnity:

> She comes! she comes! the sable Throne behold
> Of *Night* Primaeval, and of *Chaos* old!

One would hardly suppose from those alone that anything remotely comic could follow. There is good reason for this solemnity. For all the humour that *The Dunciad* contains, Pope is at bottom deadly serious. If he ridiculed fools, it was because he valued and indeed possessed the kind of true intelligence, as opposed to fake 'cleverness' and trivial accomplishment, that could mercilessly see into and devastatingly lay bare the extent and nature of their imbecility. For him the approach of *Dulness* was a genuine overthrow of what may be called the intellectual commonwealth, a deadly blow dealt at the comity of sensitive and intelligent human beings.

Hard upon the portentousness of the opening couplet comes something of quite a different kind:

> Before her, *Fancy's* gilded clouds decay,
> And all its varying Rain-bows die away.

Fancy may be decaying, but the effect of the lines which tell us this is that of a brightly sensuous, if rather superficial attractiveness, which merges into the firework-display suggested by the next couplet:

> *Wit* shoots in vain its momentary fires,
> The meteor drops, and in a flash expires.

To that succeeds the solemn note of the opening, with an extended, classically inspired simile in the true epic style:

As one by one, at dread Medea's strain,
The sick'ning stars fade off th'ethereal plain;
As Argus' eyes by Hermes' wand opprest,
Clos'd one by one to everlasting rest;
Thus at her felt approach, and secret might,
Art after *Art* goes out, and all is Night.

The last line, though, tells us that this is no ordinary epic vision, but rather a monstrous allegory of intellectual extinction, which comes to take on more and more the character of a nightmare. It is hard to know whether one should laugh or mourn at the spectacle of

'skulking *Truth* to her old Cavern fled,
Mountains of Casuistry heap'd o'er her head!'

Truth has always been inclined to evade man, but only because man, in pursuit of her, has only succeeded in chasing her away and burying her finally in pretentious and sophistical arguments. Similarly, Pope's succinct account of the fate of Philosophy (shunning the idea of a divine 'first cause' behind creation as being 'unphilosophical') is both a devastatingly compressed summing up of the pass to which Philosophy has been led, in the poet's opinion, by certain thinkers, and a ludicrously grotesque picture. There is the same mixture of the intensely serious and the richly absurd in the vision of complete intellectual turmoil in the lines which follow:

Physic of *Metaphysic* begs defence,
And *Metaphysic* calls for aid on *Sense*!
See *Mystery* to *Mathematics* fly!
In vain! they gaze, turn giddy, rave, and die.

But the catastrophe is not a solely intellectual one; the anarchy extends to the fields of religion and morality. Neither a publicly shared faith, nor a privately held rule of life independent of religious considerations, is possible any longer:

Nor *public* Flame, nor *private*, dares to shine;
Nor *human* Spark is left, nor Glimpse *divine*!

Thus the stage is set for the grand finale, where the conventionally awe-inspiring and sublime reverberation is tempered with the witty notion of the whole thing being like the Creation in reverse. 'Let there be darkness!' decrees 'CHAOS', and the curtain falls impressively on the restoration of '*Night* Primaeval'.

Something remains to be said about the use of the prevailing imagery in this passage—the imagery of Light versus Dark. Basically, Light is here associated with all that *Dulness* overthrows, and Dark with the Goddess herself. But Pope discriminates between the different things with which Light is associated. He by no means attaches the same value to all of them. The 'gilded clouds', for instance, suggest a decidedly critical view of '*Fancy*'. It may be superficially attractive, but in reality it is rather false and meretricious, like the surface gilding that covers something quite commonplace and insubstantial. The firework-display of *Wit*, for all its brightness, is soon over; the meteor which drops and expires so soon is not really a meteor at all, but merely a rocket.

If Pope laughs away the claims of *Fancy* and *Wit*, he is, however, in earnest when he comes to 'the sickening stars', for they are the Arts which, one by one, are extinguished by the approach of *Dulness*. '*Art* after *Art* goes out, and all is Night' is deadly serious. Something that is genuinely valued is here being annihilated.

'Light dies before thy uncreating word' is one of the great lines in the English language. Apart from the reference to Genesis already noted, it suggests that the 'word' of *Dulness* is the epitome of all that is written and said by false poets, critics, philosophers, and hacks and frauds of all kinds, and that this 'word' kills the truth and the intelligence.

THE NINETEENTH CENTURY

The following short poem is so familiar from anthologies, that many readers must have felt a twinge of impatience on finding it reappearing in this book. There is a good reason for including it, however, and readers are asked to overcome the faint aversion which familiarity may have brought.

She dwelt among the untrodden ways
    Beside the springs of Dove,
A maid whom there were none to praise,
    And very few to love.

A violet by a mossy stone
    Half-hidden from the eye!
Fair as a star, when only one
    Is shining in the sky.

She lived unknown, and few could know
    When Lucy ceased to be;
But she is in her grave, and, oh,
    The difference to me!

WILLIAM WORDSWORTH

This poem has suffered the fate of a great deal of heavily anthologized verse—the fate of being much read but little understood. For this tiny poem, like so much of Wordsworth, is simple only in appearance. Its language is so lucid and 'ordinary', that once the reader has found that the Dove is a river in the north of England, there would seem to be no obstacle to understanding. Surely Wordsworth is merely telling us that there was once a maid called Lucy, who lived in a remote place, who had a certain type of unostentatious beauty, and who is now dead. He certainly is telling us these things, but there is more to the whole business than at first meets the eye.

If the reader tries to forget that he has ever come across this poem before, he will find that concentration upon the meaning, upon what the words are actually saying, raises two interesting points. Consider first of all the opening lines of the final stanza:

She lived unknown, and few could know
    When Lucy ceased to be;

One may have read those lines many times without stopping to examine their precise significance. For a curious problem here arises with regard to the words 'unknown' and 'know'. If Lucy really did live 'unknown', in what way is it possible to suppose that even 'few' could 'know' the time of her death? Taken in the most literal sense, the lines are absurd, since nobody at all could know when a genuinely unknown person 'ceased to be'. It is obvious, then, that as Wordsworth presumably does not mean to be absurd, he must be using the verb 'to know' in two different senses. What he is saying may be clumsily explained as follows: Lucy was a person who lived quite without any kind of renown ('She lived unknown'). When she died, only a few people could have been aware of the event.

There is, however, more to be said about the lines in the light of what we are told in the first stanza:

> A maid whom there were none to praise,
> And very few to love.

Understanding of Wordsworth's meaning depends upon a sharp distinction between 'none', and 'very few'. It is all too easy to blur this distinction, and read the lines as though Wordsworth had said 'A maid whom there were *few* to praise'. Such a lazy construction of his words will not do. 'None', and 'very few', mean two entirely different things, and unless we grasp the exact nature of the difference between them in this context, we shall not be within a hundred miles of properly understanding the poem. Wordsworth is telling us that although there were indeed a 'very few' people who loved Lucy, those few did not ever think of *praising* her. He is quite definite about this—'A maid whom there were *none* to praise'. The love of these people for Lucy, then, seems not to have involved feeling that she had any special distinction.

Reasons for this are given in the second stanza. Her beauty was of a singularly inconspicuous type, like the beauty of a solitary violet barely visible beside 'a mossy stone'; or like the beauty of one single star, which would never be noticed in a sky full of other glinting points of light.

Now, the question arises whether the poet himself is or is not to be included among the 'very few' who loved Lucy without thinking her worthy of praise. The more obvious interpretation would be that he is the solitary exception, that he, of course, valued Lucy at her true worth all along. The last stanza might seem to suggest this:

She lived unknown, and few could know
When Lucy ceased to be;
But she is in her grave, and, oh,
The difference to me!

Wordsworth, according to this interpretation, is singling himself out. The 'few' who knew the time of Lucy's death are doubtless the 'very few' who loved her, or at any rate include those persons. And the poet might appear to be telling us that he alone was genuinely affected by the event. In that case it must be assumed that her death makes such a 'difference' to him precisely because his regard for her has always been of a unique kind. The second stanza would thus be taken as expressing the 'praise' which he was the sole person to bestow upon her.

Another interpretation, however, is not only possible, but even more probable. I have said that Wordsworth is quite definite about there having been *none* to praise Lucy. If he says 'none' he must be allowed to mean it. If we give full weight to this 'none', we are forced to conclude that the poet himself is to be counted among the people who loved Lucy without praising her. It is now that the words 'She lived unknown' begin to sound with a new reverberation. Emphasis comes to be placed on '*lived*', and the words can be interpreted as meaning not only that she lived without any kind of renown, but that *while she was alive she was not really known by anybody, including the poet, for what she truly was.* It is only now that she is dead, now that what was taken for granted has vanished from the familiar scene, that he realizes the value of what he has lost.

Some readers may object that a poem which can be given two such interpretations cannot be said to have used language with precision. To an objection of that kind, the best reply is that precision does not necessarily involve meaning one thing and one thing only. The poet is concerned here with a human experience, a human experience of more complexity than appears at first sight. To make us feel the full force of the experience, he packs as much meaning as he can into an extremely small space. That this compression leaves us guessing

about the poet's valuation of Lucy while she was alive is not to be
accounted a weakness, since a degree of uncertainty on this score is
itself part of the experience that the poem sets out to communicate.
The ambiguity of the poem, therefore, paradoxically does make for
precision, as it is a means of putting the experience before the reader
as fully and disturbingly as possible.

*   *   *

To Autumn

Season of mists and mellow fruitfulness!
  Close bosom-friend of the maturing sun;
Conspiring with him how to load and bless
  With fruit the vines that round the thatch-eaves run;
To bend with apples the moss'd cottage-trees,
  And fill all fruit with ripeness to the core;
    To swell the gourd, and plump the hazel shells
  With a sweet kernel; to set budding more,
And still more, later flowers for the bees,
Until they think warm days will never cease,
    For Summer has o'er-brimm'd their clammy cells.

Who hath not seen thee oft amid thy store?
  Sometimes whoever seeks abroad may find
Thee sitting careless on a granary floor,
  Thy hair soft-lifted by the winnowing wind;
Or on a half-reap'd furrow sound asleep,
  Drowsed with the fumes of poppies, while thy hook
    Spares the next swath and all its twined flowers;
And sometimes like a gleaner thou dost keep
  Steady thy laden head across a brook;
  Or by a cider-press, with patient look,
    Thou watchest the last oozings, hours by hours.

Where are the songs of Spring? Ay, where are they?
  Think not of them, thou hast thy music too,
  While barred clouds bloom the soft-dying day,
And touch the stubble-plains with rosy hue;
  Then in a wailful choir the small gnats mourn
  Among the river sallows, borne aloft
    Or sinking as the light wind lives or dies;

And full-grown lambs loud bleat from hilly bourn;
Hedge-crickets sing; and now with treble soft
The redbreast whistles from a garden-croft,
And gathering swallows twitter in the skies.

JOHN KEATS

'Here at last', the reader may say to himself, 'is a poem which really does fit in with my ideas of what poetry ought to be. No disconcerting wit, no peculiar and unfamiliar blend of intellect and emotion—nothing but three nice comfortable stanzas about Nature, which, as I have so often been told, is above all subjects the one most suited to poetry.' Possibly some readers will feel offended at seeing their capacities rated so low. If that is so, their indulgence is begged; but they are at the same time asked to reflect on the still widespread view that certain topics, amongst which Nature stands pre-eminent, are intrinsically 'poetic', whilst others are not. General critical opinion long since turned its back upon such a notion, yet answers to examination questions very often reveal that it is continuing to echo round many a classroom, doing its bad old work of alienating the intelligent pupil from poetry.

This is not the place to attempt a historical explanation of how this view came to be current. What does need to be said, however, is that there is no reason why any subject under the sun should not be made into poetry. Poetry, like prose, is a way of using language. The fact that it generally makes play with certain devices not normally found in prose has nothing whatever to do with the poet's choice of subject. He is at perfect liberty to write about Nature if he wants to, but his selection of that topic will not in itself make his work 'poetic'. Thus the poem we have before us does not rank as a fine poetic achievement because of its subject-matter. If we praise it, we do so because of the splendid vitality with which Keats writes. To be sure, this can and should make us more aware of sights and sounds in the landscape with which we are personally familiar, whether they are similar to those of Keats or totally different; but this quickening of response to everyday experience may be brought

167

about through poems on a wide variety of subjects, of which Nature is only one.

Many readers of this book will never have experienced the season of autumn in Europe. Little or no disadvantage attaches to this, as far as Keats's poem is concerned. Indeed, the ode evokes the sights and sounds of autumn so vividly that it is a more than adequate substitute for first-hand knowledge of the season. All that the reader needs to bear in mind, when approaching the poem, are the facts that (*a*) autumn comes between the warm season of summer and the cold season of winter, and that (*b*) it is the season of harvest, when everything has reached complete fruition.

The first line of the poem really sums up the character of the season in a nutshell. If autumn is the season of 'mellow fruitfulness', it is also the season of 'mists'. With the warmth of the 'maturing sun' there goes a suggestion of chill, like a distant warning of the winter to come. Yet the general impression of this stanza is that of a steady, benevolent warmth, radiating out from the second line, in which autumn and the sun are for a moment personified and thought of as friends on terms of the warmest intimacy. Notice that the word 'maturing' can be taken in two ways. Its most obvious sense is that the sun, through its warmth, is maturing the fruits of the earth. The sun is thus the agent which brings about the general ripeness. But the word can also be made to apply directly to the sun itself. Like the fruit which it ripens, the sun is reaching full maturity, a final fruition which must soon give way to the dearth and cold of winter.

The rich abundance of the season is suggested by the cumulative effect of the language: 'mellow fruitfulness', 'maturing sun', 'load and bless', 'To bend with apples', 'fill all fruit with ripeness to the core', 'To swell the gourd', 'plump', 'more, And still more', 'o'er-brimm'd'. These words act upon one another and upon us in such a way that we, like the bees, are tempted to think that 'warm days will never cease'.

In the second stanza autumn is again personified, this time in the shape of a series of persons whose activities (or absence of them) are particularly associated with the season. First we have a man sitting on the floor of a granary, 'careless' probably because the work has been done and the storehouse is full. Then comes a slumbering reaper, sent to sleep by the heavy scent of the poppies growing among the corn, the furrow on which he was engaged only half finished, his hook lying idle and sparing, till he wakes, the next swath of corn and the flowers twining around the stalks. Observe how the impression of heavy drowsiness is conveyed by the movement. The articulation of the words 'a half-reap'd furrow' has a retarding effect, and the stress on 'Drowsed', with its prolonged vowel, almost brings the movement to a standstill.

More interesting, however, is the enactment of meaning in the line 'Spares the next swath and all its twined flowers'. It will be noted that articulation is again rather difficult, so that part of the effect will be to intensify the feeling of drowsiness already generated. But that is not the whole story. If the reader will examine his oral sensations as he reads the line aloud, he will find that they have an even more 'tongue-twisting' character than was given by Donne's line 'I dare not move my dim eyes any way'. And what, after all, could be more in keeping? The tongue seems to twist and twine in the mouth, just as the flowers are tangled and entwined in the corn. It is worth pointing back to a similar effect in the first stanza—'the vines that round the thatch-eaves run'. Here we have the same kind of analogy between the movements of the mouth and the growth of a vine, which, like all creeping plants, loves to twine itself around the objects against which it grows.

Autumn is next visualized as a gleaner, who picks up what is left behind in the cornfield, here and there, when it has been reaped and the crop carted away. His head laden with his gatherings, he is seen carefully steadying his load as he steps across a small stream. In his book *Revaluation*, F. R. Leavis has shown how Keats uses his verse-structure here to enact the movement of the gleaner. The reader 'steps' across from 'keep' to 'Steady' in the next line, as the gleaner steps across the brook. And in the necessary pause after 'keep' (quite a decided one, for it is a rhyme-word), we have a suggestion of the momentary hesitation of the gleaner as he balances his load before crossing. The last two lines of the stanza, in which autumn is imagined as watching the apple-juice slowly trickling from a cider-press crushing the fruit to pulp, display the same sense of the potentialities of language. The extreme difficulty of saying with any clarity 'Thou watchest the last oozings', suggests the almost painful slowness with which the drops of juice appear.

If the first two stanzas have concentrated upon the sights of autumn, it is to the typical sounds of the season that we now turn. Keats tells us that it is vain to regret the passing of 'the songs of Spring', for autumn has its own characteristic 'music'. Two points call for particular attention here. One comes in the middle of the stanza, where the poet speaks of the sound made by 'the small gnats'

> borne aloft
> Or sinking as the light wind lives or dies.

The voice rises at the end of the line on the word 'aloft', and falls on 'sinking', thus exactly enacting the meaning. Our second point concerns the last line: 'And gathering swallows twitter in the skies'. We noted that the very first line of the poem contains a hint of coming chill, in the word 'mists'. It is appropriate that the poem should end with the same kind of premonition. If the swallows are gathering, it is because they are preparing to migrate to warmer climes, now that winter is fast approaching.

✳ ✳ ✳

The reader may justifiably feel that this account of the poem has not gone quite far enough, that something has been left out. And indeed the poem is more than just an evocation of the autumn atmosphere. Implicit throughout is a deeper theme, the theme of Life and Death. The way in which this theme is treated is highly characteristic of Keats. In another poem, the *Ode on Melancholy*, Keats tells us that Melancholy

> dwells with Beauty—Beauty that must die;
> And Joy, whose hand is ever at his lips
> Bidding adieu;

Both Beauty and Joy are here thought of as carrying with them the inevitability of their own passing, an inevitability of which one is aware at the very moment of contemplating the one or experiencing the other. Something similar is going on in the *Autumn* Ode. The first stanza gives an impression of richly abundant life, of triumphant maturity. Yet, as the slight shudder of chill in 'mists' indicates, this cannot last for ever. It is just as impermanent as Beauty and Joy. With the third stanza, the suggested approach of Winter, 'the soft-dying day', and the bare expanses of the now reaped 'stubble-fields', hint in different ways at the prospect of death once the human individual has reached, and left behind, the phase of full maturity, physical and intellectual. Yet Keats does not make this an occasion for sorrow. The 'music' of autumn, even of this late phase, has its own character. The inevitable prospect of death is not something to be shunned or artificially hidden. Rather, it is something to be serenely accepted as part of the very business of being alive, para-doxical though this may seem.

It will be observed that Keats nowhere makes his 'message' explicit in the poem. And yet the poem indisputably has this pro-found moral significance, all the more powerfully felt for not being cast in the form of a sermon.

✳   ✳   ✳

> With blackest moss the flower-plots
>   Were thickly crusted, one and all:
> The rusted nails fell from the knots
>   That held the pear to the gable-wall.
> The broken sheds look'd sad and strange:
>   Unlifted was the clinking latch;
>   Weeded and worn the ancient thatch
> Upon the lonely moated grange.
>   She only said, 'My life is dreary,
>   He cometh not,' she said;
>   She said, 'I am aweary, aweary,
>   I would that I were dead!'

✳   ✳   ✳

About a stone-cast from the wall
A sluice with blacken'd waters slept,
And o'er it many, round and small,
The cluster'd marish mosses crept.
Hard by a poplar shook alway,
All silver-green with gnarled bark:
For leagues no other tree did mark
The level waste, the rounding gray.
She only said, 'My life is dreary,
He cometh not,' she said;
She said, 'I am aweary, aweary,
I would that I were dead!'

＊　　　＊　　　＊

The sparrow's chirrup on the roof,
The slow clock ticking, and the sound
Which to the wooing wind aloof
The poplar made, did all confound
Her sense; but most she loathed the hour
When the thick-moted sunbeam lay
Athwart the chambers, and the day
Was sloping toward his western bower.
Then, said she, 'I am very dreary,
He will not come,' she said;
She wept, 'I am aweary, aweary,
Oh God, that I were dead!'

ALFRED LORD TENNYSON

These stanzas have been selected from a poem called *Mariana*. It is quite frankly an exercise in building up 'atmosphere', an atmosphere suggested to the poet by four words which occur in Shakespeare's *Measure for Measure*—'Mariana in the moated grange'. The poem presents us with the situation of a woman alone in a derelict house, waiting with diminishing hope, from day to day, for deliverance from her solitary captivity. Tennyson does not explain why she is in the moated grange, or why she needs one particular man to deliver her. We are at liberty to imagine any story we please. The poet's concern is to create an impression of overwhelming dreariness and desolation, and he exploits language most skilfully to this end.

The most obvious feature of the poem is the refrain at the end of each stanza. A reading of the words aloud will show how artfully Tennyson has contrived that the movement should be slow, heavy, and clogged—suggestive, indeed, of the woman's very feeling of unutterable weariness with life. But the poem contains things which are more subtle and interesting than that. Take the opening lines:

> With blackest moss the flower-plots
> Were thickly crusted, one and all:

The reader may be wondering why the effect of thick encrustation should be brought home to him so extremely vividly. The explanation lies in the articulation of the words, especially 'blackest moss' and 'thickly crusted'. Clear enunciation of them involves some care and deliberation, resulting in a leaden-footed movement. That in itself would not account for the peculiar felicity of the lines, however, as it has no relevant application to their meaning. What does call for comment is that the effort of articulation, which gives rise to this movement, gives the reader a sense of *oral impediment*. The sounds seem to be hanging heavily in his mouth, thickly encrusting his tongue, so to speak, just as the flower-plots are thickly crusted with moss.

In the second stanza quoted, we can observe the same kind of enactment of meaning:

> About a stone-cast from the wall
> A sluice with blacken'd waters slept,
> And o'er it many, round and small,
> The cluster'd marish mosses crept.

Again it is the movement that counts. Articulation of the second line is not easy, if the words are to be brought out distinctly, mainly because of the predominance of sibilants. There is consequently a dull lifelessness about the movement, perfectly consonant with the still, stagnant water's imagined appearance. As for the fourth line, the clustering of the mosses on the surface is suggested by the packed clustering of consonants, as experimental reading aloud will demonstrate.

Such effects of enactment, as we pointed out in a previous chapter, can be included under the heading of imagery. Our third stanza provides a good example of a more familiar type of imagery—onomatopoeia:

and the sound
Which to the wooing wind aloof
The poplar made.

Here the very sound of the wind in the solitary tree seems to sigh through the words. Most readers will be quick to detect and appreciate the use of onomatopoeia, but fewer are likely to notice at once what is happening later in the stanza:

but most she loathed the hour
When the thick-moted sunbeam lay
Athwart the chambers, and the day
Was sloping toward his western bower.

The first thing to interest us in these lines is the sunbeam, slanting across the chambers as the sun sinks lower in the western sky towards the close of day. To suggest the light, so conspicuous because so heavily loaded with the dust of the derelict house, striking across the rooms, Tennyson uses a device to which the reader should by now have grown accustomed: playing off the run of the sense against the verse-structure. In the transition from the second to the third of the lines quoted, the meaning is literally made to lie 'Athwart' the verse-structure. Due attention to the line-ending at the word 'day' will produce a heavy stress on 'sloping', with an effect of expiring energy; and this is appropriate not only to the sinking of the sun, but also to the weariness expressed with overwhelming grief and despair in the modified version of the refrain with which the poem closes.

✳ ✳ ✳

Dover Beach

The sea is calm to-night.
The tide is full, the moon lies fair
Upon the straits;—on the French coast the light
Gleams and is gone; the cliffs of England stand,

Glimmering and vast, out in the tranquil bay.
Come to the window, sweet is the night-air!
Only, from the long line of spray
Where the sea meets the moon-blanch'd land,
Listen! you hear the grating roar
Of pebbles which the waves draw back, and fling,
At their return, up the high strand,
Begin, and cease, and then again begin,
With tremulous cadence slow, and bring
The eternal note of sadness in.

Sophocles long ago
Heard it on the Aegean, and it brought
Into his mind the turbid ebb and flow
Of human misery; we
Find also in the sound a thought,
Hearing it by this distant northern sea.

The Sea of Faith
Was once, too, at the full, and round earth's shore
Lay like the folds of a bright girdle furl'd.
But now I only hear
Its melancholy, long, withdrawing roar,
Retreating, to the breath
Of the night-wind, down the vast edges drear
And naked shingles of the world.

Ah, love, let us be true
To one another! for the world, which seems
To lie before us like a land of dreams,
So various, so beautiful, so new,
Hath really neither joy, nor love, nor light,
Nor certitude, nor peace, nor help for pain;
And we are here as on a darkling plain
Swept with confused alarms of struggle and flight,
Where ignorant armies clash by night.

MATTHEW ARNOLD

Dover Beach, first published in 1867, is a very typical utterance of its period. With the spread of scientific discovery and knowledge, there had set in, among thinking people in England, a profound scepticism with regard to religious orthodoxies which had for generations gone unchallenged. For some men this meant downright rejection of

traditional faith, for others a lifetime of compromise between ortho-
doxy and sceptical inquiry. There was indeed a fundamental unrest
beneath the confident surface of the Victorian age, with its material
prosperity and its apparent air of complacent security.

Matthew Arnold's poem is put together with remarkable skill.
No one would guess from the opening what the central theme is to
be; yet, when it does explicitly appear, it comes with a sense of
perfect inevitability, so carefully worked out is the overall design.
The first six lines create an atmosphere of utter serenity, with 'calm',
'fair', 'tranquil', and 'sweet' as the key words. It is a serenity
disturbed only momentarily—if it can really be said to be disturbed
at all—by the sudden glimpse of a light over on the coast of France,
the effect of which is suggested by the placing of the word 'Gleams'.
The gentle but nevertheless decided way in which the reader 'leans',
as it were, on this word, conveys the impression of the light briefly
shining out, to be quickly extinguished in the three rapidly uttered
words 'and is gone'.

With 'Only', which, again, is carefully placed so as to receive
maximum stress, the atmosphere begins to change. It is still a tranquil moonlit night, but there is a flaw in its perfection. As a contrast
to the preceding calm, there comes a new note, introduced by 'the
grating roar Of pebbles which the waves draw back,...'. Notice
how skilfully Arnold has used his verse-structure to suggest the to-
and-fro motion of the pebbles and the water. Observe particularly
the stress on 'up', which gives an almost physical sense of the
force with which the pebbles are flung on to the beach. With this
sound there enters 'The eternal note of sadness', 'eternal' because
Arnold thinks of it as being heard by every age in the history of man.

Sophocles, he says, heard the same sound long ago by the shores
of the Aegean, and the note of sadness meant for him 'the turbid ebb
and flow Of human misery'—the very stuff, in fact, of his great
tragic dramas. 'We', likewise, are led to meditation by the sound;
but whereas the tragedies of Sophocles, however great the suffering
they depict, are in their final effect very far from being merely

depressing, the 'thought' that 'we' find in the sound brings us near to gloomy despondency.

The theme of the poem now makes an explicit appearance. 'The Sea of Faith', like the English Channel lapping Dover Beach on this tranquil night, 'Was once, too, at the full'. But, unlike the sea upon which the poet has been gazing, it is ebbing, with a 'melancholy, long, withdrawing roar'—note the onomatopoeia in the last two words and the reference back to the 'grating roar' of line 9. Human beings were once able unquestioningly to *believe*; now it is becoming increasingly difficult for them to do so. Thus the eventual prospect must be that of a world utterly devoid of faith, a world as comfortless as a waste of 'naked shingles'.

If this is the prospect man faces, how is he to live? If he cannot any longer believe in the faiths which sustained generations before him, to what can he turn for support? The answer comes with the words

> Ah, love, let us be true
> To one another!

In a perfect love-relationship lies the only real possibility of security in the world. At least the lovers can be 'true', whereas 'the world', in one way or another, is one great lie. Arnold carefully places the word 'seems' at the end of a line, thus momentarily isolating it, and emphasizing the fact that what we have here *is* mere seeming. The variety, beauty, and newness of the world are illusions. Where everything 'seems' so positive and alluring, there is 'really' only a string of negations:

> neither joy, nor love, nor light,
> Nor certitude, nor peace, nor help for pain;

We have moved a long way from the mood of the opening. No longer are we gazing from the window upon the moonlit sea. We are now in a nightmare landscape of the imagination, haunted by shapes and sounds which typify the conflicts sweeping over a world in which traditional faith is fast crumbling; where men fight without really knowing what they are fighting for, or whom they are actually supposed to be attacking. Thus a poem, that has begun with the serene, unruffled movement of 'The sea is calm to-night', ends on a bitterly discordant note, the rhythm jagged and rough, the words harsh-sounding and violent:

> Where ignorant armies clash by night.

It is worth pointing out that the 'ignorant armies' are meant to be taken metaphorically. They are not actual soldiers, nor is the 'darkling plain' literally a battlefield. One has to think of them as representing conflicts and antagonisms of many different kinds—for example, political parties and creeds, social classes, nationalisms, systems of philosophy, and so on.

*   *   *

> No worst, there is none. Pitched past pitch of grief,
> More pangs will, schooled at forepangs, wilder wring.
> Comforter, where, where is your comforting?
> Mary, mother of us, where is your relief?
> My cries heave, herds-long; huddle in a main, a chief
> Woe, world-sorrow; on an age-old anvil wince and sing—
> Then lull, then leave off. Fury had shrieked 'No lingering!
> Let me be fell: force I must be brief'.
>
>   O the mind, mind has mountains; cliffs of fall
> Frightful, sheer, no-man-fathomed. Hold them cheap
> May who ne'er hung there. Nor does long our small
> Durance deal with that steep or deep. Here! creep,
> Wretch, under a comfort serves in a whirlwind: all
> Life death does end and each day dies with sleep.
>
> GERARD MANLEY HOPKINS

This sonnet is a human document as agonizing as Donne's 'Thou hast made me'. It records a mood of overwhelming despair, and one has the feeling that all the resources of poetic language are being drawn upon to make the wild grieving real and immediate to the reader.

The very first words arrest us: 'No worst, there is none'. The possibility of there being a 'worst', a point beyond which sorrow cannot go, a point where at least one might take comfort in the

178

thought that nothing more painful can possibly be in store, is here denied. As Hopkins sees it, things never get to their ultimate worst; they simply keep on growing worse. There is thus no limit to the pain sorrow can inflict. This is immediately confirmed and extended. The misery which the poet has already experienced amounts only to 'forepangs', the agonies that precede even greater sorrows, sorrows of a kind outside the scope of 'grief' as we normally understand the word. These new pangs are 'Pitched past pitch of grief' in two senses: (*a*) they are so intense that they are beyond the range of ordinary grief; (*b*) they have a 'blackness' more deep than the blackness of pitch. But the words can also be taken as applying in a different way to the poet himself. He is 'pitched up' to the point at which it seems his fortitude must finally give way, as the strings of a musical instrument will break if it is pitched up too high by being overstrung.

The third and fourth lines give an impression of the agonized, pleading, speaking voice, very similar to effects found in Donne's sonnet. Observe the tormented insistence on the word '*where*'. Hopkins feels completely lost, since his familiar sources of consolation, God and the Virgin Mary, seem to have deserted him.

In the fifth line, we find that the poet's wild 'where, where' leads to the imagined cries of a densely packed herd of cattle—or perhaps, more appropriately, a great flock of sheep—as they 'heave' forward, each animal jostling the next, until they 'huddle' together so that it is impossible to pick out individual beasts in the mass. Thus one cry comes hard upon the other. But their cries are the poet's cries as well, cries from the depth of a grief so intense that it seems to him

a chief
Woe, world-sorrow,

epitomizing all the sorrows of humanity. And not merely the sorrows of humanity at the time at which he is writing, but the sorrows of the world throughout the ages. His cries are now transformed into the noise, the 'wince and sing' of the iron being beaten on 'an age-old anvil'. There follows a moment of exhausted calm: 'Then lull, then leave off'. But the agony and the panic noise return with the shriek of Fury, reaching its height in the astonishing device used in the step from line 7 to line 8:

> 'No ling-
> ering!

This is playing off the sense against the verse-structure with a vengeance! The break is this time actually made to come in the middle of a word, not merely in the middle of a sentence. Yet the result of this bold step is superbly right. The heavy stress on the first syllable of 'lingering', necessitated by the fact that it comes at the end of the line and is required for the rhyme, conveys irresistibly the very shriek of Fury itself.

Observe the spareness and deliberate disjointedness of the syntax in the sestet. In the first four lines there is only *one* article—'the', the second word of the first line. And at the beginning of the third line we have to supply an imagined 'He' to make the sense complete. Is this not a fair representation of the way thoughts actually occur in 'the mind'?

But there is more to be said about the opening of the sestet. Look once more at the first sentence:

> O the *mind*, *mind* has *mountains*.

Here the repetition of 'mind', together with the alliteration which links the word with 'mountains', suggests a piling up of masses, peak upon peak. In the transition from 'cliffs of fall' to 'Frightful', in the next line, there is a further instance of Hopkins's assured mastery of his medium. In the pause after 'fall' there is enacted the terrified glance over the precipice to the dizzy depth below. The catch of the breath at the end of the line conveys a sense of vertigo— the poet is shrinking away from the sight of the drop—and 'Frightful' comes out with a shudder analogous to Donne's 'Such terror'.

Another point of special interest also arises from the handling of the run-on line. Hopkins is telling us that the only kind of person who can take the mind's abysses lightly is the one who has never experienced their terror:

> Hold them cheap
> May who ne'er hung there.

He, on the other hand, knows them all too well. He has most certainly 'hung there'. And the actual feeling of hanging on the edge of a precipice is given to us by the suspension of the meaning from one line into the next, as we step from 'cheap' to 'May'. The same sense of the precariousness of the hold comes with the next line-ending:

> Nor does long our small
> Durance deal with that steep or deep.

The pause after 'small' suggests a flagging of the capacity to hold, while the stress on 'Durance' conveys the desperate effort to hang on.

The abysses of the mind, in fact, open up prospects too terrifying to be contemplated for long. In sheer exhaustion, Hopkins turns away from the spectacle to the cold comfort of

> all
> Life death does end and each day dies with sleep.

It is a bitter contrast to the 'comforting' he has vainly begged in the third line of the poem.

Much could be said about the wonderful handling of rhythm in this poem. Consider from the rhythmic point of view these lines from the octave:

> My cries heave, herds-long; huddle in a main, a chief
> Woe, world-sorrow; on an age-old anvil wince and sing—
> Then lull, then leave off.

As in the Donne sonnet, but to an even greater extent, one has the impression of being positively forced through something. The alliteration in the first line, far from being musical, like Spenser's, contributes to the sweep of the rhythm as we pass through the succession 'heave, herds-long; huddle'. But to mention the 'sweep' of the rhythm is not to imply that it moves smoothly, without impediment. It is a *strenuous* sweep, and the strenuousness is communicated to the reader as he articulates the words. Notice how the first line of the passage moves irresistibly to the emphasis of 'chief', so superbly appropriate to the sense. And consider the way in which Hopkins varies the rhythm in the second and third lines. Reading aloud 'on an *age*-old *an*vil *wince* and *sing*' one has a sense of the beating of the hammer on the iron. Contrast the hammered emphasis of that with what follows: 'Then lull, then leave off'. None of these words is heavily stressed, but 'then' in each of its appearances has slightly more emphasis given to it than the other words. The effect here is that of failing energy, of drooping exhaustion.

Here is the opening poem of a sequence called *Ash Wednesday*. Ash Wednesday is the first day of the season of Lent in the Christian calendar, a season of penitence and renunciation. The title thus indicates the mood of disciplined spiritual contemplation and self-examination which prevails throughout the sequence.

> Because I do not hope to turn again
> Because I do not hope
> Because I do not hope to turn
> Desiring this man's gift and that man's scope
> I no longer strive to strive towards such things
> (Why should the agèd eagle stretch its wings?)
> Why should I mourn
> The vanished power of the usual reign?
>
> Because I do not hope to know again
> The infirm glory of the positive hour
> Because I do not think
> Because I know I shall not know
> The one veritable transitory power
> Because I cannot drink
> There, where trees flower, and springs flow, for there
>   is nothing again

Because I know that time is always time
And place is always and only place
And what is actual is actual only for one time
And only for one place
I rejoice that things are as they are and
I renounce the blessed face

And renounce the voice
Because I cannot hope to turn again
Consequently I rejoice, having to construct something
Upon which to rejoice

And pray to God to have mercy upon us
And I pray that I may forget
These matters that with myself I too much discuss
Too much explain
Because I do not hope to turn again
Let these words answer
For what is done, not to be done again
May the judgment not be too heavy upon us
Because these wings are no longer wings to fly
But merely vans to beat the air
The air which is now thoroughly small and dry
Smaller and dryer than the will
Teach us to care and not to care
Teach us to sit still.

Pray for us sinners now and at the hour of our death
Pray for us now and at the hour of our death.

T. S. ELIOT

The feature of this poem that has probably most struck the reader is the extremely sparse punctuation. In those forty-one lines there are only eight stops. This is far from being a piece of affectation, a mark of 'modern' eccentricity. It is an essential factor in the poem's success, for it controls the manner in which it is to be read. When Eliot does use punctuation marks, we shall find that their effect is very precisely calculated.

The poet is here commencing his spiritual discipline by renouncing worldly ambition, desire, even the strivings of reason. Perhaps, however, it is misleading to say that 'the poet' is doing this. For although the poem is written in the first person, the overall impression it gives is that of suppression, even voluntary annihilation, of the individual personality. The 'I' of the poem seems to be less the individuality of Thomas Stearns Eliot than an unindividualized voice speaking for all men who seek to renounce and repent. For purposes of convenience in discussion, nevertheless, we shall speak of the 'poet', asking the reader to remember that the poem is certainly not just a fragment of versified autobiography.

The preliminary avowal of renunciation, which makes up this first poem of the sequence, is cast in a form which suggests a ritual religious utterance. The absence of stops gives something of the effect of a *chant*, intoned in a flat voice from which all positive feeling has been carefully excluded. Note the differences in meaning between the first three lines. If the poet does not 'hope to turn *again*', it must be that he has 'turned' in the past. Now he does not even hope to be deflected from his chosen path of renunciation. In the second line he abandons the possibility of hope itself, for hope might tempt him by leading him to desires from which he wishes to escape. The third line returns to the idea of 'turning', but this time there is a significant change in the run of the verse. Whereas the first three lines seem completely separate from one another, there is a definite link between the third and the fourth. To 'turn' would involve 'Desiring' things which have been renounced, and in the transition from the third line to the fourth there is the sense of a momentary wistful glance over the shoulder back to the ambitions that are being left behind. But this faint suggestion of regret is quickly dispelled. The fifth line, with its weary, awkward movement, stresses the futility of striving for 'such things', and the two questions that follow reinforce this feeling. (Notice that the question-marks here, after the absence of punctuation, have an effect of affirmation rather than doubt.)

When punctuation marks reappear in the next group of lines, they again have a very definite function. The process of renunciation has continued; the poet does not hope any more to have the fleeting experience of triumphant mastery that comes with the 'positive hour'. A 'glory' it may seem to be at the time; but it is 'infirm', because it is glory as the world knows it, and therefore merely 'transitory'. Not only personal glory, but the stimulus and refreshment that are drawn from the natural world, are eternally given up:

> Because I cannot drink
> There, where trees flower, and springs flow, for there
> is nothing again

Yet the difficulty of acknowledging that he 'cannot drink' is conveyed by the manner in which the verse is made to move. The stress on 'There' suggests a vividness, a sense of the precise, particular quality of what is being renounced, quite distinct from the flat monotone of the lines leading up to it. And this vividness of realization persists through the next six words—'where trees flower, and springs flow'. The poet no longer seems to be chanting, but eagerly evoking the alluring charm of the sensuously beautiful world; almost, as it were, catching his breath with each comma, as his mind harks back to all that freshness and life. The sudden quickening of life does not last, however. The vision is an illusion, seductive though it may be, and the line peters out on a note of utter negation: 'for there is nothing again'.

If the poet has been in danger of swerving from the path of renunciation in this line, his balance is more than set right in what follows. Time, place, and the limitations associated with them, are flatly accepted for what they are. No more does he say 'I *do not hope* to turn again'. The words are now 'I *cannot hope*'. And with this recognition of the hopelessness of hoping comes a kind of wry happiness, born out of the necessity of finding something to be happy about, now that so much has been given up:

> Consequently I rejoice, having to construct something
> Upon which to rejoice

From here onwards the poem takes on more and more the character of a prayer. With the lines 'And pray to God to have mercy upon us', and 'May the judgment not be too heavy upon us', the liturgical

185

flavour given by the purposely flat, unpunctuated verse grows more pronounced. (Though it should be noted that the second of those lines may be as much an appeal to the charitable judgment of the world as to the mercy of God. If we take that line with the two succeeding ones, it can be regarded as a plea to the world not to look too harshly on the poet's lack of vitality—vitality, of course, as the world sees it.) Yet there is one positive fact that emerges. 'The air... is now thoroughly small and dry', and it is 'Smaller and dryer *than the will*'. Perhaps that is not saying much, but at least the *will*, whatever else may be feeble or even non-existent, continues to possess *some* vestige of strength, even though it is perhaps almost as 'small and dry' as the air. The will, on the other hand, precisely because it still retains some vigour, might conceivably be a source of disturbance for the poet's mood of renunciation. The will to renounce could possibly change, despite his protestation that he 'cannot hope to turn', to the will to hanker after the very things he is abandoning. It is for this reason that he calls upon God to

> Teach us to care and not to care
> Teach us to sit still.

This is by no means mere word-spinning. We should be taught to 'care' in the sense of caring for the pursuit of the kind of intense spiritual discipline with which the poem is concerned; and in learning to 'care' in such a manner, we shall also learn 'not to care' for the allurements, be they ambitions, desires, or whatever, of the non-spiritual world. To learn how 'to sit *still*', quelling the impulses towards vain striving which may from time to time threaten our pursuit of renunciation, is the simply stated yet certainly not easily attainable object of the whole discipline.

After 'still' there comes, appropriately, a full stop, and the poem ends on a formal note stressing its connection with the Lenten period of repentance:

> Pray for us sinners now and at the hour of our death
> Pray for us now and at the hour of our death.

For some, perhaps many, readers, the attitudes which find voice in *Ash Wednesday* may be unpalatable. Two points might be useful in bringing them into touch with the poem: (*a*) the need to renounce something, and to start life afresh, can come to those who do not share Eliot's Christian beliefs, or indeed the beliefs of any religion at all; (*b*) whatever the extent of agreement or disagreement with the attitudes expressed, the poem, in its turning away from what we normally consider to be 'life', is paradoxically *full of life*. The very flatness of tone at which it aims, varied occasionally and strikingly by spare punctuation, is itself, strangely enough, the product of a sense of the resources of language that is far from moribund. Though it seems to turn its back upon vitality, it could never have been written without that concern for language as a precision tool which is the life-blood of literature.

SHAKESPEARE: A POSTSCRIPT AND AN EXERCISE

Many readers will probably have wondered why a book about understanding literature should have made so little mention of the greatest of writers in English. The reason is that Shakespeare is too large a subject to receive summary treatment, and that the kind of large-scale attention he demands at the level we have kept in mind throughout this book has been accorded to him elsewhere.[1]

The reader is invited, however, to consider the following passage from *Macbeth*, Act III, Scene ii, in the light (*a*) of our discussion of poetry in this and the previous chapter, and (*b*) of our approach to the organization of Dickens's *Bleak House*:

MACBETH. Be innocent of the knowledge, dearest chuck,
　　　　　Till thou applaud the deed. Come, seeling Night,
　　　　　Scarf up the tender eye of pitiful Day,
　　　　　And, with thy bloody and invisible hand,
　　　　　Cancel, and tear to pieces, that great bond
　　　　　Which keeps me pale!—Light thickens; and the crow

---

[1] Notably in *Understanding Shakespeare*, by E. F. C. Ludowyk (Cambridge, 1962).

Makes wing to th'rooky wood;
Good things of Day begin to droop and drowse,
Whiles Night's black agents to their preys do rouse.
Thou marvell'st at my words: but hold thee still;
Things bad begun make strong themselves by ill.
So, pr'ythee, go with me.

Macbeth has plotted the murder of Banquo, but only half reveals his intention to Lady Macbeth. The reader should concentrate particularly upon the words 'seeling Night', 'pitiful Day', 'bloody and invisible hand', 'that great bond', and the line 'Good things of Day begin to droop and drowse'. He should endeavour to relate them, and the associations they conjure up, to things said and done elsewhere in the play, as well as seeing the cumulative effect they produce in the context in which they are uttered. When the reader is able to do this with confidence, when he is capable of placing a key-passage with a sense both of its local significance and its meaning in the total design of the work to which it belongs, he may justifiably tell himself that his claims to 'understand literature' are not vain.

INDEX